D1632348

The tributaries of the Ganges, which needed to be crossed during the 1980 Himalayan Rally, are wide and rapid. Here Indian natives carry the Young/Jones Minor, formerly owned by the Archbishop of Canterbury, on poles at shoulder height. (Copyright Philip Young)

MORRIS
MINOR & 1000
ohv SALOONS, TRAVELLERS & CONVERTIBLES

Ray Newell

CONTENTS

Foulis

Haynes

Titles in the *Super Profile* series

Ferrari 250GTO (F308)

Jaguar Mk 2 Saloons (F307)

Lotus Elan (F330)

MGB (F305)

Morris Minor & 1000 (ohv) (F331)

Porsche 911 Carrera (F311)

Further titles in this series will be published at regular intervals. For information on new titles please contact your bookseller or write to the publisher.

ISBN 0 85429 331 0

A FOULIS Motoring Book

First published 1982

© **Haynes Publishing Group**
All rights reserved. No part of this book may be reproduced or transmitted in any form or by any means, electronic or mechanical, including photocopying, recording or by any information storage or retrieval system, without written permission from the publisher.

Published by:
Haynes Publishing Group
Sparkford, Yeovil,
Somerset BA22 7JJ

Distributed in USA by:
Haynes Publications Inc.
861 Lawrence Drive, Newbury
Park, California 91320, USA

Editor: Rod Grainger
Dust jacket design: Rowland Smith
Page layout: Barry Griffiths
Printed in England by: J.H.Haynes &
Co. Ltd.

FOREWORD

The postwar Morris Minor is assured of a place in motoring history on the basis of its sales record alone. More significantly though, it has secured for itself a place in the affections of people throughout the world and this, along with its reputation as a well designed, economical and reliable form of transport, will go some way to ensuring that the "Morris" name will be remembered long after B.L. finally cease to use it on their cars.

In many ways the Morris Minor is enjoying a new lease of life even though production ceased over a decade ago. Supported by a thriving club scene and a healthy spare parts situation, owners, enthusiasts and collectors alike find it a practical proposition to own and maintain a Morris Minor.

One of the most pleasant things about writing this book has been the opportunity it has afforded me to meet with, and learn from, fellow owners and enthusiasts.

Essentially this small publication concentrates on the Saloon, Traveller and Convertible models of the Morris Minor range which were fitted with Overhead Valve (ohv) engines, though in the interests of achieving a true historical perspective of the development of these particular vehicles, earlier models and prototypes are considered briefly. Within the pages that follow there should be something of interest for everyone whether they are Morris Minor owners or not. The picture gallery amongst other things, provides a visual insight into the development of the various models while the "Owner's View" divulges the opinions of selected owners about their cars. For the technically minded there are contemporary road test reports, specifications for each model and a production evolution section, and for the intending buyer there are some hints and tips on what to look for as well as additional information on clubs, specialists and books.

In the course of collating information many people have made valuable contributions and I would like to acknowledge the assistance of: Paul Davies and Zelda Cohen of the Morris Minor Owners Club for their help in providing photographs and contemporary literature; Peter Gamble and Michael Moore of the same club who have assisted with my technical queries; Rick Feibusch Editor of *Minor News,* the Joint American Club magazine, who provided me with a wealth of information; Pat Carlsson and Jim Funnell who submitted to my questions for the Owner's View and who, along with Philip Young, Editor of *Sporting Cars* and David Burrows, provided me with superb pictures and information about their respective motorsport activities; and Anders Clausager of B.L. Heritage who painstakingly sorted out numerous photographs and checked out technical and production details.

I am also grateful to *Autocar* and *Motor* magazines who were helpful in allowing the reproduction of their respective contemporary road tests on various Morris Minors and to Paul Skilleter, who, apart from taking most of the pictures in the photo gallery, has given me every encouragement in writing this book.

A special thank you must go to all those people who put their magnificent cars at my disposal for the photographic session and who took so much trouble preparing their cars before, and on the day.

Finally, I would like to thank Sue Hardy whose help in typing the manuscript has been invaluable and Roy Turner who has worked so hard, providing me with photographs, often at short notice.

Ray Newell

HISTORY

Family Tree

The Motor Show held in Earls Court, London in 1948 was an historic occasion, not only because it was the first show of its kind to take place in Britain for ten years due to the outbreak of the Second World War, but because many of the cars present heralded a new era in motoring design and engineering.

None did so more than the range of Morris Cars which made their first public appearance at the show. The Morris Oxford, Morris Six and Morris Minor were accurately described by *The Autocar* as "entirely new cars". Yet the names given to the new models belied their innovative nature and kept alive familiar Morris names.

"Modern descendant of a famous ancestor" was how *The Autocar* regarded the new Morris Oxford. With its modern lines, unitary contruction, independent front suspension, column gearchange and 1476cc sidevalve engine, it was a long way from the first 2-seater car which William Morris produced in 1913 and to which he gave the name Morris Oxford. It was a long way too, from the 'Bullnose' and 'Flatnose' Oxfords and Cowleys of the 20s which helped launch a career which would see William Morris, later Lord Nuffield, acknowledged as the most successful British car

manufacturer of the inter war years.

The 1948 Morris Six Series M.S. carried on the tradition of 'Sixes' the most successful of which was the 2.5-litre overhead camshaft-engined 1928 model. The postwar version with its 2.2-litre six cylinder overhead camshaft engine shared mechanical and some styling features with the Six Eighty Wolseley which was announced at the same time. It continued in production until 1954 by which time 12,465 had been produced.

Morris Minor was not a new name either. Morris Motors had produced an overhead valve 847cc model called the Morris Minor in 1929, following their takeover of the Wolseley company. The intention was to produce a model to rival the best selling Austin Seven and thus to secure a foothold in the small car market. Though the car sold reasonably well it never seriously rivalled the Austin Seven — in spite of a £100 price tag in 1930. The Wolsley-derived overhead camshaft engine, regarded by some as too sophisticated for the Morris Minor, was replaced by a simpler sidevalve unit in 1931. This engine remained in use until production ceased in 1934, by which time hydraulic brakes and a four-speed synchromesh gearbox had been introduced. It is interesting to note that the discarded overhead camshaft engine continued to be used in a slightly modified form along with the Morris Minor chassis in the first M.G. Midget — the M type.

If the first Morris Minor had not attained all the success that had been hoped for, then its postwar successor was destined to make up for it and put the name Morris Minor firmly in the record books. Few would have predicted in 1948 that the new Morris Minor — the baby of the range — would be the first British car to break the million sales barrier, or that it would enjoy a production run of

twenty-two years! It was fitting that it should have been another best-selling Morris car that retained the most direct link with the post-war Morris Minor.

The Morris Eight, introduced in 1934 and subsequently updated with Series II and Series E models, used a 918cc sidevalve engine. It was the redesigned version of this unit introduced in 1938 and used in the updated Series E that was to provide the element of continuity when, ten years later, it was decided to use the same engine in the Morris Minor Series M.M. Four years later, following the merger between the Austin Motor Co. Ltd. and Morris Motors Ltd. to form B.M.C., the Morris Minor would once again be powered by an ohv engine — thus bridging the gap between pre-war and postwar Morris Minors.

In purely social terms there was in Britain a need, in the immediate post war years, for a small, practical and economical family car. In harsh economic terms there was a desperate need for a successful British-made car which would boost export sales. The Nuffield Organisation Publicity Department, in reviewing the factors relating to the development of the Morris Minor on the occasion of the launch of the 'special edition' in 1961 to mark the millionth Morris Minor built, noted the following additional factors: "... the exceptional smoothness of British roads, the conservative cornering habits of domestic drivers and the fact that fewer than one car in ten was shipped overseas all conspired to produce a climate of opinion in which the public would buy archaic designs of chassis so that standards of comfort then available in America were far ahead of anything to be had in the U.K. and the levels of steering, cornering power and road holding normal in England could not be compared with those established in Europe. For example, when war broke out in 1939 only two British small cars had combined body and chassis construction, only two had independent front wheel suspension, none had both and none had rack and pinion steering.'' It was against this background and under the direction of Miles Thomas (later to become Lord Thomas) that Alec Issigonis (later Sir Alec) set about designing a new small car.

Concept and Design

Issigonis's brief was to produce a small saloon which could go into production soon after the war. In retrospect it can be seen that Issigonis, the young and talented designer, had very clear cut ideas about the form the new vehicle should take. This is borne out by his early sketches which bear an uncanny resemblance to the first production model and by the fact that his influence was not confined to one aspect of the car's design. The whole concept of the car was his and though he had able assistants in Jack Daniels and Reg Job, Issigonis was directly involved in the ideas behind the car's unitary construction, its styling details, the steering and suspension layout and even an experimental engine.

Most of his ideas were embodied in the first experimental prototype, the Mosquito, which emerged in December 1943. Some were revolutionary and did not meet with universal approval within the then recently formed Nuffield Organisation. Apart from its striking design which prompted Lord Nuffield to refer to it as a ''poached egg'', the outstanding features of the new model were its monocoque construction, rack and pinion steering, independent front suspension incorporating torsion bar springs and 14 inch wheels. Some of the subsequent prototypes, there were eight in all, were powered by an experimental

flat four water-cooled engine using a three speed gearbox with column gearchange: during testing, 800cc and 1100cc versions were tried. This engine was favoured by Issigonis and Daniels and remained a serious contender for inclusion in production vehicles until a late date, but it was eventually dropped in favour of the well tried and tested — and more importantly, readily available — 918cc Series E sidevalve engine which had been used in the Morris 8.

Production

It was with these late changes, and as the Morris Minor and not the Mosquito, that the new model went into production during 1948. The sidevalve engines and corresponding gearboxes were made by Morris Engines Ltd of Coventry but the later ohv units fitted from 1952, following the creation of B.M.C., came from Longbridge. Bodyshells, comprising of 834 different parts, were manufactured in Birmingham at Nuffield Metal Products Ltd. and final assembly took place at Cowley.

Demand for the vehicles had clearly been underestimated initially and two new assembly tracks had to be laid down in a new building at Cowley within a year of the first car being produced. This in itself is a measure of how well the new model was received. Both the Saloon and the Tourer models were enthusiastically welcomed at the Motor Show and in the motoring press — outshining even their more expensive contemporaries such as the Hillman Minx and the Jowett Javelin.

The Autocar's considered opinion was, ''A very large section of the car using public in this country of narrow roads, small

garages and minimum petrol supply is waiting patiently for a new small car like this and now that it is made it is beyond expectations.'' The car may well have been made but for many the patient wait was not over, for export requirements took priority over home market sales and even in 1952 when the four door model was announced the situation had changed very little.

The ''New Morris Minor'' was billed as the ''World's Supreme Small Car'' in the early publicity material. In listing its many virtues it was claimed that it was the only small car in the world that embodied big car features. The emphasis on overseas markets is clearly evident and the chart shows how successful the export drive was in the early years. The Series II model introduced in 1952 wasn't significantly different in body style to the earlier Series M.M. but its mechanical components were the first tangible signs of the merger which had taken place in 1952 between the Nuffield Organisation and the Austin Motor Company to form B.M.C. (British Motor Corporation Ltd). At the 1951 Motor Show, Austin *had* announced the A30, their new small car — designed to rival the Morris Minor. It was powered by an 803cc overhead valve engine later to be designated the ''A-series'': it was this engine that was fitted to the Series II Morris Minor range.

1953 saw the introduction of the first Morris Minor commercial vehicles and the Traveller model. A year later a restyled Series II range appeared and prompted the publicity to say: ''New look for world's biggest small car buy''. The Series II continued in production until 1956 when it was replaced by the much more modern-looking Morris 1000 range. Powered by a much better 948cc engine and more compatible transmission this model sold well both at home and abroad. By December 1960 it was estimated that a million Morris Minors — in all its guises — had been sold and to mark the occasion a "Special Edition" of Minor *Millions* was produced. These cars were standard 948cc 2 door saloons, but certain special trim features were added. These included, lilac paintwork, off-white upholstery with contrasting piping, special side bonnet badges and rear boot badge denoting "Morris 1,000,000" and special wheel rim embellishers. These cars were launched in a blaze of publicity marking what was, then, a significant achievement in British motoring.

In September 1962 the final Series of Morris Minors was announced. Considerable restyling had taken place and a larger 1098cc engine was fitted. With some modifications this model continued in production until questions began to be asked about the viability of continuing to produce Morris Minors.

In spite of the emphasis on exports, surprisingly few concessions were made in terms of styling and special export features during the production life of the Morris Minor range, (lefthand-drive excluded). There were of course certain statutory lighting requirements which had to be met. In the case of export models for the United States of America flashing indicators were fitted as early as 1952, and blanking plates covered the semaphore indicator slots. On later models, fresh air heaters were available on export models before they became available as standard equipment on U.K. models. Additional optional extras were whitewall tyres and reclining seats.

Reasons for Discontinuation

During the late 1960s Morris Minor sales declined steadily. In 1968, when Leyland and B.M.C. merged

to form British Leyland, production had dropped to 31,640 for that year. Many people felt that as a result of the merger Lord Stokes would discontinue production of the Morris Minor immediately. However it was not until June of the following year that the first step in phasing out the Morris Minor took place when the last convertible was produced.

Competition was fierce in the late 60s, even within the newly formed British Leyland group the Minor faced stiff competition from the new Austin Maxi and more importantly from the popular Austin/Morris 1100/1300 range. With plans advanced for a new Morris model — the Marina — it seemed only a matter of time before production would finally cease at Cowley. The grim realisation that profit margin on each Morris Minor produced in 1968 was in single figures, coupled with a diminishing sales market, resulted in production of saloons being discontinued at Cowley on the 12th November 1970 in order to make way for the new Marina production lines. In April of the following year the last traveller was assembled at the Morris Commercial Cars Plant at Adderley Park, Birmingham, thus bringing to an end a production run for the Morris Minor which spanned twenty-two years.

Motorsport

The Morris Minor appears at first to be an unlikely contender for any serious motorsport event yet, since their inception in 1948, Morris Minors *have* been involved in competition at all levels including International Rallying.

Of the models featured in this book the Series II fared worst as far as motorsport success was concerned. In standard form the Series II was hopelessly slow and

was handicapped by wide gear ratios and a disadvantageous power to weight ratio — factors which still combine to make them unpopular choices for Classic Saloon Car Club racing.

When the new 948cc Morris 1000 was announced in 1956, B.M.C. once again looked at the possibilities of becoming involved in International rallying. The improved A-series engine, accompanying gearbox and higher ratio back axle gave rise to optimism that the Minor could at last compete on favourable terms with its rivals. With B.M.C. backing, the dynamic duo of Pat Moss (Carlsson) and Anne Wisdom (Riley) dominated the rally scene in the late fifties, scoring many successes in a variety of cars. Their exploits in "Grannie", their Morris 1000 Saloon, were exceptional and did much to raise confidence in the Morris 1000 following the lack of success recorded by Series II models. They competed in all the major International rallies, except the Alpine, and finished in all but one — the Monte Carlo. They notched up a number of stunning results including a 4th place overall in the R.A.C. Rally of 1958, and numerous 1st and 2nd places in the *Coupe des Dames* which culminated in their winning the European Ladies Championship in 1958.

Pat still enthuses about the Minors she rallied and is impressed by their reliability. She is quick to pay tribute to those who worked to 'build' their car and keep it going — particularly Nobby Hall. Nevertheless she points out the limitations of the car and gives an insight into why it was not more successful. "With the restrictions on what modifications you could make, the Minor was basically overweight and underpowered. The brakes weren't good — much better with Riley or disc brakes fitted — and there was a fair amount of axle tramp".

No significant achievements

were recorded in the 1960s as it was left to private individuals to race and rally Minors. Indeed it was not until 1980 that a Morris Minor emerged from International competition with honour and distinction. Philip Young, then Editor of *Collector's Car* and the Rev. Rupert Jones, former International rally driver and noted A35 long distance record holder, entered the Himalayan Rally. Their choice of vehicle was a 1967 Morris 1000 saloon which had been owned by the Archbishop of Canterbury. With the assistance of Nobby Hall, who had worked on Pat Moss's Minor, a 1275cc engine with many Sprite/Midget components was built. Philip takes up the story, ''The chassis was standard as far as any strengthening goes apart from the 'skidding' of the rear spring hangers and a dural sumpshield. Extra instruments were a dual water temperature/oil gauge given by Abingdon and which was in fact an M.G.B. instrument taken out of the dash of a TR7 driven by Timo Makinen. A second-hand pair of seatbelts were scrounged from an ex-Tony Pond TR7. The car could do a 'ton' on the standard axle ratio, the close ratio gears were super and we caned it non-stop. It handled very well indeed thanks to its 165x14 Avon Artic Steels, and bearing in mind it started in 67th place and rose to 9th, overtaking more cars than anyone else, to win the small car class, it did exceptionally well. I reckon it was all down to the agile dimensions of the Minor and its truly unburstable feel.

''The Rev. Rupert Jones didn't make one mistake on the maps and showed remarkable stamina, particularly at the end when he drove the car out of the mountains . . . he drove the last stage when the brakes failed and slid the car up a dry stone wall to slow her down!'' The Minor finished 15th overall and won its class. The durability of car, and drivers, had been tested to the full.

In recent years Morris Minors have featured in many of the Classic Saloon car races and in the categories for modified vehicles. Class wins are not uncommon and David Burrows was the Winner of Class D in the Pre-57 Saloon Car Championship of Gt. Britain, competing against A35s, Fiat 500s and Standard 10s amongst others. In 1979 he was the overall Championship Winner, fending off challenges from Jaguars, Zephyrs and M.G. Magnettes.

Thus the Minor has had its share of sporting success to add to the other successes considered in the next section.

Success Review

Judging the success of any car is a difficult task and, in the case of the Morris Minor, it is made doubly so by the fact that it has become a well loved and much admired vehicle. Personal feelings can cloud one's judgement but by almost any criteria one wishes to apply the Morris Minor *is* a success story.

In terms of sales, the total number sold over a production span of twenty-two years bears little relation to the volume sales of today, but the Morris Minor was the first British car to reach the million sales barrier and the total sales figure of all types including commercials of 1,619,857 was creditable by any standard.

The export drive, so essential to the British economy in the immediate postwar years, was a success and by 1960 479,525 vehicles had been exported, a staggering total of 48% of the total produced. The boom years for exports to the United States were 1957-61 when, according to Rick Feibusch editor of *Minor News,* (the joint publication of the American Morris Minor Clubs), 45,218 948cc Morris 1000s were sold. The significance of this figure

is only appreciated when one realises that up to the time exports to the United States ceased, in 1967, total sales in the U.S. were just under 57,000.

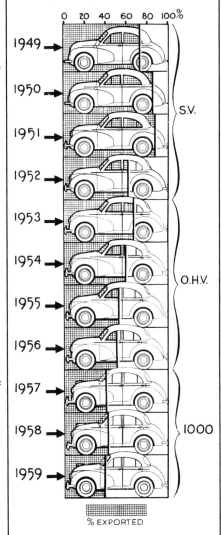

Chart showing Morris Minor export performance as issued by the Nuffield Organisation in January 1961. (B.L.Heritage.)

The extent of the worldwide sales is surprising with the top ten markets up to 1960 being:

Australia . . . . 101,246 cars
U.S.A. . . . . 52,431 cars
Eire . . . . 35,492 cars
South Africa . . . . 34,639 cars
New Zealand . . . . 34,216 cars
Canada . . . . 29,538 cars
Sweden . . . . 25,375 cars
Holland . . . . 20,356 cars
Malaya . . . . 16,405 cars
Denmark . . . . 14,213 cars

In terms of design the car owes much to the flair and brilliance of Sir Alec Issigonis. His revolutionary design features have stood the test of time and even allowing for the updating production changes it is a testimony to his design and engineering skills that the successors to the car he conceived in the early 1940s are not out of place on British roads today.

As a functional economical family car the Morris Minor was a success too. The range of vehicles, Saloons, Tourers, Travellers and commercials catered for most motoring needs. Easy maintenance, cheap, easily available spares and low running costs all contributed to the appeal of the Minor during its production life. Like other cars they had rust problems but it is significant that they lasted better than many of their contemporaries.

The development of one-make clubs and the establishment of many specialist firms in the post production era reflect continuing

interest in the model and will no doubt ensure that the Morris Minor, already viewed by some as a postwar classic car, remains 'on the road'.

Only time will tell whether as a 'classic' car the success story of the Morris Minor will continue . . .

EVOLUTION

The *Car (Chassis) Number* appears on the identification plate which is mounted on the righthand side of the dash panel next to the main wiring harness grommet aperture. The practice of recording *Engine Numbers* changed throughout production. On very early models the engine number was stamped on a disc attached to the flywheel housing, it also appeared on the identification plate. On other models the engine number was stamped on a plate secured to the righthand side of the cylinder block above the dynamo mounting bracket, it also appeared on the identification plate. On 1098cc models it only appeared on the cylinder block.

From April 1952 until September 1962 Car (Chassis) Numbers were prefixed by an *Identification Code* consisting of three letters and two numbers. The first letter indicates the make and model (F = Morris Minor); the second letter indicates the body type (e.g. A = 4 door saloon, B = 2 door saloon); the third letter indicates the colour in which the vehicle is finished (e.g. A = Black); the first number indicates the class to which the vehicle belongs (e.g. 1 = R.H.D. Home Market, 2 = R.H.D. Export); the second number indicates the type of paint used to finish the vehicle (e.g. 1 = Synthetic, 2 = Synobel,

3 = Cellulose). Thus: FBA13 = Morris Minor, 2 door saloon, black, produced as righthand-drive for the home market and finished in cellulose paint. Note: The second number denoting paint type was not always used on later models.

From September 1962 until production ended a different *Car Number Identification Code* prefix was used. This consisted of three letters and one figure followed by an additional letter if the vehicle differed from standard right hand drive.

The first letter donotes the make of the vehicle (M = Morris); the second letter denotes the model's engine type (A = A-series engine); the third letter denotes the body type (S = 4 door saloon, 2S = 2 door saloon, W = dual purpose, T = 4-seater tourer); the fourth prefix (a number) denotes the Series of model — indicating a major change (Post 62 vehicles 5th Series); the fifth prefix denotes vehicles which differ from standard R.H.D. (L = Lefthand drive, D = De luxe). Thus: MA2S5 = Morris 1000, righthand drive, standard 2 door saloon, fifth series. Note: Dates and car number change points are, in some cases, approximate as the manufacturers sometimes incorporated modifications before, or after, the 'official' change point. Where major production changes occurred change points have been included for all models. Elsewhere the earliest known change point is given.

Production Modifications

While production changes are detailed for ohv engine models only, it is worth noting that the first Morris Minor in production was a 2 door saloon Car No. SMM 501 and it was October 1950 when the first 4 door saloon became available and headlights were fitted

in the wings for the first time (Car No. SMM 62551).

August 1952: First ohv Engine fitted in 4 door saloon. (Sidevalve engine continued in some), 160001.
January 1953: All models fitted with ohv engine, 180001.
October 1953: New model designated 'Traveller' introduced, 216901. De luxe models introduced featuring heater, leather seats, over-riders and passenger sun visor. 2 door Saloon, 221842. 4 door Saloon, 221803. Convertible, 221914.
January 1954: 'A' type rear axle and standard swivel pin assembly introduced, 228267. Wedge type fan belt at engine no. 72610.
June 1954: Engine steady cable, 264013.
October 1954: Horizontal grill bars introduced. Revised instrument and control panel. Separate speedometer, fuel and oil pressure gauges replaced by single separate instrument with open gloveboxes each side, 286441. 2 door Saloon, 291140, 4 door Saloon 290173. Convertible, 291336. Traveller, 289687. New larger rear light fitting incorporating reflector in lens cover fitted, 293051.
August 1956: Coloured hoods fitted to Convertible, 433571.
October 1956: Series II discontinued. Final Chassis number 448714.
October 1956: Standard and De luxe two and four door Saloons. Convertible and Traveller introduced, designated "Minor 1000". 948cc engine fitted. Single piece curved windscreen and larger rear window. Dished steering wheel. Horn and trafficator control on steering column. Glovebox lids fitted. Deeper rear wings. Shorter gearlever. "Minor 1000" motif on sides of bonnet, 448801.
December 1956: New strengthened steering swivel pin assembly fitted, 462458.
March 1957: Fuel tank enlarged from 5 to 6 gallons, 487048 Saloon Traveller, 485127.

September 1957: Canvas hood on convertible replaced by plastic coated material, 524944.

November 1957: Gearlever reset and lengthened. Traveller, 552906. Other models, 557451.

October 1958: Courtesy light switches fitted in front doors, 654750.

December 1958: Rear spring design changed from 7 x ¼ inch leaves to 5 x ¼ inch leaves, 680464.

February 1959: Early type dry paper element air cleaner, car 698137. Traveller, 693918.

March 1959: Wider opening doors, self-cancelling direction indicator switch fitted to steering column. Horn button moved to centre of steering wheel. Traveller, 704254. 4 door Saloon, 705224. 2 door Saloon, 705622.

September 1959: Combined inlet and exhaust manifold. Foot space between gearbox cover and clutch pedal increased. PVC interior roof lining fitted instead of cloth. Front passenger seat on 2 door saloon and Traveller modified to give better access to rear seats, 750470.

During 1960: H.S. type S.U. Carburettor introduced. Engine No. 9 M/U/H. 353449.

January 1961: Morris Minor 1,000,000 produced as special edition of 349 cars. Special features included Lilac colour, white upholstery with black piping, "Minor 1,000,000" badging on sides of bonnet and on boot lid and special wheel rim embellishers. 1,000,000-1,000,349, (these car numbers designated out of sequence).

October 1961: Flashing direction indicators incorporated into front and rear lamps. Semaphore type direction indicators discontinued. Glove compartment lid removed. Windscreen washers fitted on De luxe models. Seatbelt anchorage

points built in to all models. New range of colours and upholstery offered. 2 door Saloon, 925555. 4 door Saloon, 925448. Convertible, 947088. Traveller, 925679.

September 1962: 948cc engine. Series discontinued. Final Chassis numbers: 2 door Saloon, 990288. 4 door Saloon, 990283. Convertible, 989679. Traveller, 990289.

April 1963: Fresh air heater introduced. Air Intake on Radiator Cowl. Redesigned windscreen washer system, 1039564.

October 1963: Windscreen wiper blades lengthened and now work in tandem. Zone toughened windscreen introduced. New design combined side/flasher lamps at front and rear. Extra round amber light fitted to rear of Traveller. New type air cleaner fitted to prevent carburettor icing in cold weather. N/S door lock fitted to 2 door models. 2 door Saloon, 1043218. 4 door Saloon, 1043752. Convertible, 1043271. Traveller, 1043226.

October 1964: New design facia panel. Better trim and more comfortable seating. Automatic boot lid support. Glovebox on passenger side fitted with lid. Combined ignition and starter switch. Other switches modified. Swivel ashtrays under parcel shelf. Crushable sun visors. Plastic rimmed interior mirror. Two spoke safety dished steering wheel. Fresh air heater performance improved. 2 door Saloon, 1082280. 4 door Saloon, 1082284. Convertible, 1082717. Traveller, 1082537.

October 1966: Sealed beam headlamps fitted. Fuse in sidelamp circuit introduced, 1159663.

October 1967: New type paper air cleaner element introduced, 1196653.

June 1969: Convertible discontinued. Final Car number 1254328.

Late 1969: Oil filter switch ceased to be fitted. Amber warning lens fitted but not used.

1970: During the last months of production some models were fitted with an alternator instead of a dynamo.

November 1970: Saloon production discontinued. Final Car numbers, 2 door saloon, 1288377. 4 door saloon, 1288299.

1971: During the last months of production some of the vehicles assembled at the Morris Commercial Cars plant at Adderley Park, Birmingham were fitted with steering column ignition locks.

April 1971: Traveller production discontinued. Final Car number 1294082.

Footnote: Reclining seats were fitted to some vehicles though they were never fitted as standard equipment.

SPECIFICATION

Please note that the specifications in each section relate to each of the models upon their introduction. For production changes see "Evolution".

Morris Minor Series II

Type   Morris Minor Series II.

Built   Cowley, England, 1952-56.
                       Total number built, 269,838.

Engine   Cast iron block and head. Pressed steel sump. Four cylinders set in line
                       with overhead valves.
    Capacity: 803cc.
    Bore & Stroke: 58mmx76mm.
    Compression: 7.2:1.
    Maximum Power: 30bhp at 4800rpm
    Maximum torque: 40lb/ft at 2400rpm
    Carburettor: Single S.U. H1 type, 1⅛in.
    Fuel pump: S.U. type L.
    Air cleaner: Dry gauze type.

Transmission   Rear wheel drive from front mounted engine. 4-speed gearbox bolted to
                       rear engine plate. Synchromesh on 2nd, 3rd and top gears. Clutch,
                       Borg and Beck 6¼in dry plate. Gear ratios: Reverse 5.174:1, First
                       4.09:1, Second 2.588:1, Third 1.679:1, Top 1.000:1. Final Drive: Hypoid
                       axle 7/37. Two pinion differential. Final drive ratio 5.286:1. Overall
                       ratio: Reverse 27.38:1, First 21.618:1, Second 13.69:1, Third 8.88:1,
                       Top 5.286:1.

Wheelbase & Track Wheelbase 7ft 2in.
                       Track — Front 4ft 2⅝in, Rear 4ft 2 5/16in.

Suspension   Front — Independent by torsion bars and links.
                       Rear — Half-elliptic leaf springs.

Steering   Rack and pinion. 2½ turns lock-to-lock.
                       Turning circle, 33ft.

Brakes	Lockheed hydraulic, 7in diameter drums.
	Front, two leading shoes.
	Rear, one leading and one trailing shoe.

Wheels & Tyres	14in pressed steel disc. 4-bolt fixings. Tyres, 5.00x14.

Bodywork	Designed by Issigonis, unitary all steel construction, assembled at Cowley. 2 door and 4 door Saloons, Convertible and Traveller available. Traveller rear section constructed with external ash frame and aluminium panelling, including roof.

Dimensions & Weight

	Overall width	Overall length	Overall height
2 door Saloon (15½cwt):	5ft 1in	12ft 4in	5ft 0in
4 door Saloon (15¾cwt):	5ft 1in	12ft 4in	5ft 0in
Convertible (15cwt):	5ft 1in	12ft 4in	5ft 0in
Traveller (16½cwt):	5ft 1in	12ft 5in	5ft 0in

Ground clearance 6¾in.

Electrical System	Positive earth, 12-volt, 43amp/hr. battery mounted on tray in engine bay. Positive earth. Lucas dynamo type C39PV/2 with Lucas compensated voltage control box and coil ignition. Headlamps Lucas double dip 42/36watt. Semaphore trafficators 3w.

Performance	Maximum speed 62mph. Maximum speed in gears: 1st 18mph, 2nd 30mph, 3rd 45mph. Accleration: 0-30 8.5 secs, 0-40 15.1 secs, 0-50 29.2 secs, 0-60 52.5 secs; standing ¼-mile 27.1 secs. Fuel consumption 36-40mpg.

Morris Minor 1000, 948cc

Type	Morris Minor 1000, 948cc.

Built	Cowley, England, 1956-62.
	Travellers were assembled at Abingdon 1960-62.
	Total number built, 554,048.

Engine	Cast iron block and head. Pressed steel sump. 4 cylinders in line, overhead valves pushrod operated.
Capacity:	948cc.
Bore & Stroke:	62.9mmx76.2mm.
Compression:	8.3:1 (High compression engine).
Maximum power:	37bhp at 4750rpm.
Maximum torque:	50lb/ft at 2500rpm.
Carburettor:	S.U. H2 type, 1¼in.
Fuel pump:	S.U. type L.
Air cleaner:	A.C. C.L. Oil Bath.

Transmission	Rear wheel drive from front mounted engine. 4-speed gearbox bolted to rear engine plate. Remote control gearchange. Synchromesh on 2nd, 3rd and top gears. Clutch, Borg and Beck 6¼in dry plate. Gear ratios: Reverse 4.664:1, First 3.628:1, Second 2.374:1, Third 1.412:1, Top 1.000:1. Final drive three quarter floating rear axle. Hypoid final drive 9/41, ratio 4.55:1. Overall ratios: Reverse 21.221:1, First 16.507:1, Second 10.802:1, Third 6.425:1, Top 4.555:1.

Wheelbase & Track	Wheelbase 7ft 2in. Track — Front 4ft 2⅝in, Rear 4ft 2$_{5/16}$in.
Suspension	Front — Independent by torsion bars and links Rear — Half-elliptic leaf springs.
Steering	Rack and pinion. 2½ turns lock-to-lock. Turning circle 33ft.
Brakes	Lockhead hydraulic, 7in diameter drums. Front — two leading shoes. Rear — one leading and one trailing shoe.
Wheels & Tyres	14in pressed steel disc, 4-stud fixing. Tyres 5.00x14 tubeless.
Bodywork	Designed by Issigonis, all steel unitary construction. 2/4 door Saloons and Convertibles assembled at Cowley. Travellers assembled at Abingdon from 1960. Traveller constructed with external ash frame for rear section and aluminium panelling including roof.

Dimensions & Weight

	Overall width	Overall length	Overall height
2 door Saloon (15½cwt):	5ft 1in	12ft 4in	5ft 0in
4 door Saloon (15¾cwt):	5ft 1in	12ft 4in	5ft 0in
Convertible (15cwt):	5ft 1in	12ft 4in	5ft 0in
Traveller (16½cwt):	5ft 1in	12ft 5in	5ft 0in

Ground clearance 6¾in.

Electrical System	Positive earth 12-volt, 43amp battery mounted on tray in engine bay. Positive earth Lucas dynamo type C39PV/2 with Lucas compensated voltage control box and coil ignition. Headlamps Lucas double dip 42/36 watt. Semaphore trafficators 3w.
Performance	Maximum speed 75.1mph. Maximum speed in gears: First 23.4mph, Second 35.2mph, Third 60.5mph. Acceleration: 0-30 6.8 secs, 0-40 12.1 secs, 0-50 18.5 secs, 0-60 30.0 secs; standing ¼-mile 24.2 secs. Fuel consumption 37-44mpg.

Morris Minor 1000, 1098cc

Type	Morris Minor 1000, 1098cc.
Built	Cowley, England, 1962-71. Total number build, 303,443.
Engine	Cast iron block and head. Pressed steel sump. 4 cylinders in line, overhead valves pushrod operated.
Capacity:	1098cc.
Bore & Stroke:	64.58mmx83.72mm.
Compression:	8.5:1 (High compression engine).
Maximum power:	48bhp at 5100rpm.
Maximum torque:	60lb/ft at 2500rpm.
Carburettor:	S.U. HS2 type, 1¼in.
Fuel pump:	S.U. type L.
Air Cleaner:	Cooper dry type, with paper element.
Oil Filter:	Full-flow, with paper element.

Transmission	Rear wheel drive from front mounted engine. 4-speed gearbox bolted to rear engine plate. Remote control gear change. Synchromesh on 2nd, 3rd and top gears. Clutch 7¼in single dry plate. Gear ratios: Reverse 4.664:1, First 3.628:1, Second 2.172:1, Third 1.412:1, Top 1.000:1. Final drive: Three quarter floating rear axle hypoid final drive 9/38 ratio 4.22:1. Overall ratios: Reverse 19.665:1, First 15.276:1, Second 9.169:1, Third 5.950:1, Top 4.220:1.
Wheelbase & Track	Wheelbase 7ft 2in. Track — Front 4ft 2⅝in, Rear 4ft 2$_{5/16}$in.
Suspension	Front — Independent by torsion bars and links. Rear — Half-elliptic leaf springs.
Steering	Rack and pinion. 2½ turns lock-to-lock. Turning circle 33ft.
Brakes	Lockheed hydraulic. Front 8in diameter drums. Rear 7in diameter drums. Front, two leading shoes. Rear, one leading shoe, one trailing shoe.
Wheels & Tyres	14in pressed steel disc. 4-stud fixing. Tyres 5.20x14 tubeless.
Bodywork	Designed by Issigonis, all steel unitary construction. 2/4 door Saloons and Convertibles assembled at Cowley. 1962-64 Travellers assembled at Abingdon. Production then transferred to Morris Commercial Cars plant, Adderley Park, Birmingham. Traveller constructed with external ash frame for rear section and aluminium panelling including roof.

Dimensions & Weight

	Overall width	Overall length	Overall height
2 door Saloon (15½ cwt):	5ft 1in	12ft 4in	5ft 0in
4 door Saloon (15¾ cwt):	5ft 1in	12ft 4in	5ft 0in
Convertible (15cwt):	5ft 1in	12ft 4in	5ft 0in
Traveller (16½ cwt):	5ft 1in	12ft 5in	5ft 0in

Ground clearance 6¾in.

Electrical System	Positive earth, 12-volt 43amp/hr. battery mounted on tray in engine bay. Positive earth Lucas dynamo type C40-1 with Lucas control box RB106/2 and coil ignition Lucas LA12. Flashing indicator unit Lucas FL5. Headlamps Lucas double dip 42/36 watts.
Performance	Maximum speed 78mph. Maximum speed in gears: First 27.5mph, Second 41.5mph, Third 68mph. Accleration: 0-30 6.4 secs, 0-40 9.8 secs, 0-50 15.8 secs, 0-60 24.2 secs; standing ¼-mile 22.9 secs. Fuel consumption 40-45mpg.

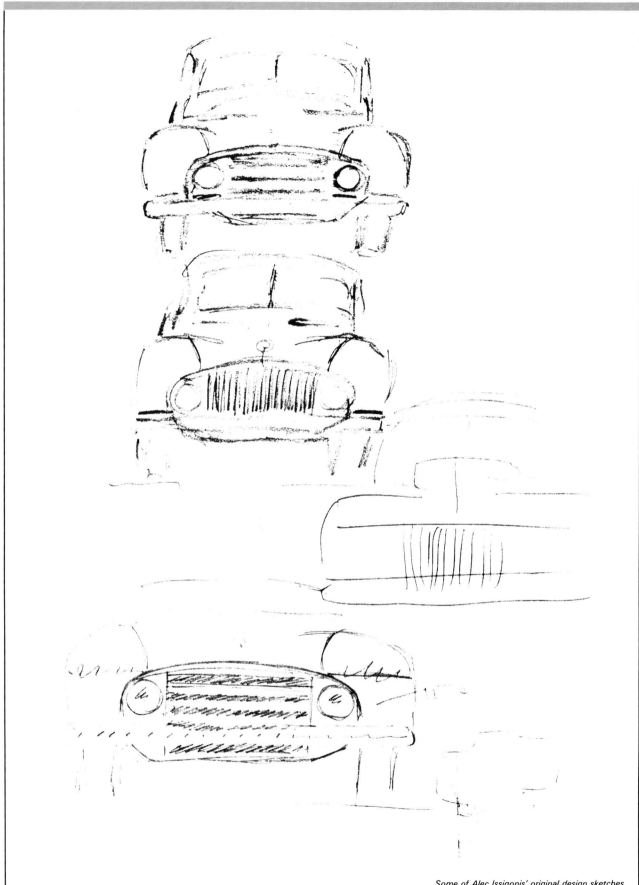

Some of Alec Issigonis' original design sketches for the Minor. (B.L.Heritage.)

THE AUTOCAR, NOVEMBER 28, 1952

1579

The Autocar ROAD TESTS

The Series II Minor is a very well-balanced car. It is a combination of functional body and chassis design, yet has character. The bonnet joint line has been modified so that it now blends into the door hinge line.

No. 1481: MORRIS MINOR SERIES II FOUR-DOOR SALOON

SINCE its introduction, the Morris Minor has firmly established itself as a popular and successful small car, and has been road tested by *The Autocar* as a two-door saloon, as an open tourer and as a four-door saloon. It has always been comfortable, well planned and nicely finished, with a commendable attention to detail, and has shown road holding and handling qualities remarkable in a vehicle of such a handy size. There is a saying that if a thing looks right it is right, and there is every suggestion of its applying to the Minor. The car is very well proportioned, and for its size has ample wheelbase and track. These two important dimensions influence the whole design of the car, for if they are correctly chosen, the designer can seat the passengers *in* the car as distinct from *on* it. Further, he can carry them within the wheelbase, and once the inter-axle seating, coupled with the "wheel at each corner" theme is realized, it is not difficult to understand the reasons for the Minor's extremely good road manners.

Recently the four-door saloon has been equipped for export with a British Motor Corporation overhead valve engine, replacing the former side valve unit, and the need to examine the effects of the new engine on performance, has provided a welcome opportunity of renewing acquaintance with this admirable small car. The overhead valve engine has a smaller swept volume than the side valve unit (800 c.c. against 918 c.c.), but it is capable of revving faster and delivers an ultimate maximum of 30 b.h.p. at 4,800 r.p.m. as against 27.5 b.h.p. at 4,400 r.p.m. for the side valve engine. Maximum torque is slightly increased and is delivered at the same r.p.m., but to allow the overhead valve engine to exhibit its full capabilities the axle ratio has been changed from 4.55 to 5.286 to 1, and consequently the engine is now turning over faster.

——— PERFORMANCE ———

MORRIS MINOR SERIES II FOUR-DOOR SALOON

ACCELERATION : from constant speeds. Speed, Gear Ratios and time in sec.

M.P.H.	5.286 to 1	8.88 to 1	13.69 to 1	21.618 to 1
10—30	..	16.1	10.0	—	—
20—40	..	17.8	12.4	—	—
30—50	..	23.5	—	—	—

From rest through gears to :

M.P.H.		sec.
30	..	8.4
50	..	25.7

Standing quarter mile, 26.9 sec.

SPEEDS ON GEARS :

Gear		M.P.H. (normal and max.)	K.P.H. (normal and max.)
Top	(mean)	62	99.8
	(best)	62	99.8
3rd	.. ..	34—42	55—68
2nd	.. ..	20—28	32—45
1st	.. ..	12—18	19—29

TRACTIVE RESISTANCE : 17.5 lb per ton at 10 M.P.H.

SPEEDOMETER CORRECTION : M.P.H.

Car speedometer	..	..	..	..	10	20	30	40	50	60	65
True speed	..	..	..	..	10	19	29.5	39	48	58	62

TRACTIVE EFFORT :

	Pull (lb per ton)	Equivalent Gradient
Top	150	1 in 14.9
Third	230	1 in 9.7
Second	350	1 in 6.3

BRAKES :

Efficiency	Pedal Pressure (lb)
77 per cent	110
75 per cent	100
43 per cent	50

FUEL CONSUMPTION :

36.25 m.p.g. overall for 262 miles (7.8 litres per 100 km.)

Approximate normal range 36–40 m.p.g. (7.9–7.1 litres per 100 km.)

Fuel, British Pool.

WEATHER : Damp surface ; slight cross wind.

Air temperature, 34 degrees F.

Acceleration figures are the means of several runs in opposite directions.

Tractive effort and resistance obtained by Tapley meter.

Model described in *The Autocar* of October 10, 1952.

———DATA———

PRICE (basic), with four-door saloon body, £405.
British purchase tax, £226 10s.
Total (in Great Britain), £631 10s.
Extras : Radio £25 2s 6d.
Heater £10 10s 0d.

ENGINE : Capacity : 800 c.c. (49 cu in).
Number of cylinders : 4.
Bore and stroke : 58 × 76 mm (2.28 × 3.00 in).
Valve gear : overhead, with rockers and push rods.
Compression ratio : 7.2 to 1.
B.H.P. : 30 at 4,800 r.p.m. (B.H.P. per ton laden, 30.9).
Torque : 40 lb ft at 2,400 r.p.m.
M.P.H. per 1,000 r.p.m. on top gear, 13.06.

WEIGHT (with 5 gals fuel), 15¾ cwt (1,778 lb).
Weight distribution (per cent) 51½ F ; 48½ R.
Laden as tested : 19½ cwt (2,178 lb).
Lb per c.c. (laden) : 2.72.

BRAKES : Type : F, Two-leading shoe.
R, Leading and trailing.
Method of operation : F, Hydraulic. R, Hydraulic.
Drum dimensions : F, 7in diameter, 1.22in wide. R, 7in diameter, 1.22in wide.
Lining area : F, 31.9 sq in. R, 31.9 sq in. (65.6 sq in per ton laden).

TYRES : 5.00—14in.
Pressures (lb per sq in) : F, 22. R, 24.

TANK CAPACITY : 5 Imperial gallons.
Oil sump, 6⅜ pints.
Cooling system, 14¼ pints (plus 1 pint if heater is fitted).

TURNING CIRCLE : 32ft 11in (L). 33ft 1in (R).
Steering wheel turns (lock to lock) : 2⅓.

DIMENSIONS : Wheelbase 7ft 2in.
Track : 4ft 2⅝in (F) ; 4ft 2⅝in (R).
Length (overall) : 12ft 4in.
Height : 5ft 0in.
Width : 5ft 1in.
Ground clearance : 6½in.
Frontal area : 18½ sq ft (approx.).

ELECTRICAL SYSTEM : 12-volt, 38-ampère-hour battery.
Head lights : Double dip, 42–36 watt.

SUSPENSION : Front, independent by torsion bars and links.
Rear, Half-elliptic springs.

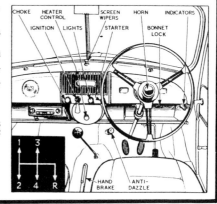

THE AUTOCAR, NOVEMBER 28, 1952

As seen from this angle the car has smooth, clean lines. The front wings run back into the front door panels, whilst the rear door finishes at the junction of the rear wing. External hinges are fitted to both bonnet and luggage locker.

Side lights are mounted on each side of the radiator grille and the head lights are flared into the wings.

ROAD TEST . . . . continued

Performance tests show that the maximum speed is little changed, the latest car showing an improvement of 1 m.p.h. in the mean figures, but there is a considerable improvement in acceleration times both on the gears and through the gears. For example, acceleration from 10 to 30 m.p.h., on top gear now takes just over 16 sec as compared with 23.5 sec with the side valve engine. At the same time, there is, however, a slight drop in the maximum speeds obtainable on the gears; the maximum normally used on third is now about 34 m.p.h., with an ultimate possibility of 42·m.p.h., whereas with the side valve engine the figures were 38 and 46 m.p.h. respectively.

The new power unit is lighter and appears more compact than the old one, so that the weight of the car unladen is now reduced by some 14 lb and there is an appreciable change in the weight distribution, the concentration of weight on the front wheels being reduced.

It may be asked how all this affects the feel of the car from the average owner's point of view. In the form now tested, the Minor is smooth and very pleasant to drive and the small engine is a very willing worker. Anyone familiar with the previous versions will immediately notice a new liveliness and an improvement in the pick up in top gear. On Pool fuel, the engine shows no signs of pinking, and although it is necessary to rev the engine fairly fast if the ultimate performance is desired, for normal motoring it will do much of its work on top gear and the car can be cruised

at near maximum without the engine becoming unduly obtrusive. The power unit is quite quiet mechanically at ordinary speeds, but a certain amount of engine noise is noticeable when it is driven hard.

As one would expect with an engine of this size, the gear box is definitely there to be used, particularly when the car is fully laden. The ratios are well chosen, with a first gear providing an overall ratio of over 21 to 1. This will, of course, cater for the Minor fully laden on the steepest of hills. In top gear it has a good measure of climbing power, but third gear is often advantageous on some of the normal type of main road hills, particularly if the driver is in a hurry. The four-speed gear box is controlled by a central gear lever, which is well positioned and very light to operate. Synchromesh is fitted on second, third and top gears; the mechanism has a pleasant, light feel. It is possible to beat the synchromesh if the driver is really in a hurry, but the unit proves completely effective in normal operation. The clutch is smooth in operation, yet the pedal operation is pleasantly light, and the pedal travel is not excessive.

There are few cars of its size that can equal the Minor for stability and road holding, which is of a very high order indeed. Handling characteristics are further improved by the use of rack and pinion steering and an independent front suspension system using torsion bars and links. The result is a vehicle that handles and steers with precision; it quickly inspires confidence and in a very short space of time the

The interior is simply yet tastefully trimmed. There is a useful shelf running below the facia and pulls are fitted to both front doors. If a radio is fitted it is placed below the glove locker to the left side of the heater unit as seen in this illustration.

The rear seat is of useful proportions, and additional comfort and convenience are provided by combined arm rests and door pulls on the rear doors. The glass in the rear side windows is divided to increase the extent to which the forward section can be lowered.

The luggage locker has a useful capacity. A separate lower compartment contains the spare wheel and tools. There is a valance between the bumper and the rear body panel.

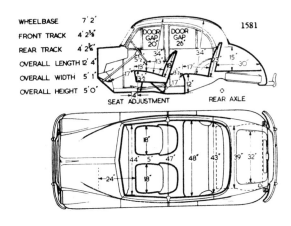

WHEELBASE 7' 2"
FRONT TRACK 4' 2⅜"
REAR TRACK 4' 2⅜"
OVERALL LENGTH 12' 4"
OVERALL WIDTH 5' 1"
OVERALL HEIGHT 5' 0"

1581

SEAT ADJUSTMENT   REAR AXLE

Measurements in these ⅛in to 1ft scale body diagrams are taken with the driving seat in the central position of fore and aft adjustment and with the seat cushions uncompressed.

driver feels completely at home in the car. There is no vagueness in the steering; it is beautifully light and positive, and does not transmit road shocks back through the steering wheel. It has good self-centring action, and, briefly, it is a steering layout that would be very difficult to improve upon. Both one up and fully laden the Minor rides well. It is in no way harsh, yet it is not in the least floppy; some slight pitching was noticed but there is very little roll on corners, and the directional stability is also good.

The hydraulically operated brakes are well up to their job, and even under the severe conditions of performance testing no fade was experienced, yet it should be recorded that on several occasions they showed a tendency to grab on the first few applications after the car had been standing for some time. This effect disappeared after a short distance. The conventional lever type of hand brake control is very well placed between the front seats, and has a sufficient leverage to enable the rear wheels to be locked.

As one would expect from the general layout of the car, the driving position is very good. The angle of the steering wheel and the position of the pedals are both well chosen in relation to one another, yet for a tall driver a slightly greater range of seat adjustment would be advantageous. The seat itself is well shaped and very comfortable, particularly when it is remembered that in a small car the weight of these components must be strictly watched. The layout of the pedals and of the dip switch is very satisfactory. Also there is little or no obstruction from the central tunnel and in consequence there is plenty of room for the driver's left foot when it is not operating the controls. The front wheel arches project into the body on the extreme sides of the toe board, forming a useful steady for the driver's right foot.

Outward visibility generally is very satisfactory. This is particularly noticeable in manœuvring and reversing because of the good three-quarter rear visibility resulting from the use of large windows in the rear doors. The driver has a clear view of the road ahead, but it is not possible to see the left-hand wing on a right-hand drive car, and the right-hand screen pillar is sufficiently wide to be obstructive at times.

Minor controls and instruments are kept to the minimum. The instrument panel contains only a speedometer, fuel gauge and oil pressure gauge—in other words, just those instruments that really matter. Above the switches is mounted an indicator light to show when the head lights are in the undipped position, while the ignition warning light is mounted above the speedometer. In a similar position on the opposite side of the facia is a button which releases the lid of the glove locker. An ash tray for the rear passengers is conveniently placed on the central tunnel just behind the front seats. Other items of equipment include twin sun vizors and an interior light.

Detail changes noted since the previous four-door saloon

was tested include a central ash tray in the facia, a more robust direction indicator switch and the use of a plastic medallion on the glove box lid in place of the former chromium and enamel ornament. The instrument panel is automatically illuminated when the side lamps are switched on and there is also a discreet green glow to show the position of the ignition switch.

The car tested was fitted with both radio and heater (optional extras). The heater unit both warmed the interior and de-misted the windows very effectively, but it did seem that a larger range of control of heater outlet air temperature would be desirable, for in this country, with the heater at minimum position, there was some tendency for the interior to become too hot, yet if the heater was switched off it quickly became cold. Double dipping head lights are fitted on this model; they have adequate range and a good spread of light and are well up to the requirements of the car. On the other hand, the horn does not seem to be quite in keeping with the high standard of the rest of the vehicle. Starting from cold was at all times very good and very little use of the mixture control was required.

The Morris Minor is a very attractive small car for those who require a vehicle that is compact, economical, very manœuvrable, and, above all, very pleasant to drive. With the latest engine it displays an increased liveliness which will appeal to many owners, particularly those who do much of their motoring on roads where there is heavy traffic.

The neat overhead valve engine is dwarfed by its auxiliaries. A large air cleaner is mounted above the engine and supplies air to the S.U. carburettor, which is fed with fuel by an electric pump located to the right of the battery, as seen in the illustration. The coil and the electrical regulator unit are mounted on the left of the bulkhead (as seen in this view), while on the extreme right is part of the radio equipment. Oil and water fillers are conveniently placed.

September 16, 1959   157   THE MOTOR

The Morris Minor 1000
Convertible de luxe

A Well-tried Open Car which Makes Low-cost Motoring a Pleasure

IMPROVED gradually over quite a long period of years, the Morris Minor is an extremely familiar-looking car which nevertheless can still provide one surprise for anyone who has not driven a recent example. The surprise comes in finding that, although newer small-car designs such as the transverse-engined Mini-Minor have brought a progressive rise in standards of comparison, this old-established model is still immensely competitive whether it be judged by measurable performance, by carrying capacity and running cost, or by those hard-to-define qualities which distinguish pleasure motoring from mere transport.

In its layout, the Morris Minor has changed little with the passing years, the most obvious difference being that a 948 c.c. overhead-valve engine developing 37 b.h.p. occupies the position which ten years ago accommodated a 918 c.c., side-valve unit of 27-b.h.p. output. In its details, however, there have been very numerous refinements, and since 1956 when we last tested a Minor 1000 a few visible changes such as a smartened-up facia have been introduced. Slightly closer study reveals that there is now a button conventionally placed at the centre of the steering wheel to sound a powerful horn, a self-cancelling fingertip switch for the turn indicators, ducting to lead fresh air to the interior heater and to distribute the warmed air more evenly within the car, and other valuable detail touches of this nature.

Economical Performance

Of a shape which is no longer fashionable but which cleaves through the air quite easily, this two-door four-seat convertible model is wide enough to give its full complement of passengers genuinely comfortable elbow-room, long enough to give four men reasonable leg-room, and provided with a conveniently arranged luggage 'locker of quite useful size. It accelerates two people and some test equipment from rest to 50 m.p.h. in 16.0 sec., or from 20 to 40 m.p.h. in top gear in 14.6 sec., reaching a top speed in excess of 73 m.p.h. Quite severe testing conditions produce overall fuel economy in the 35-40 m.p.g. range and a small degree

FRESH AIR motoring for four people, in a brisk small car with excellent road manners, continues to be provided at modest purchase and running costs by the Morris Minor 1000 Convertible.

of restraint will yield at least 45 m.p.g. on long runs.

Throughout its career this model has been renowned for good handling qualities, and though it cannot be claimed that today's Minors are superior in this respect to those of a decade ago (which had flatter rear springs), there is still the same impression that if any touring car could get out of an awkward or dangerous situation such as is liable to occur unexpectedly on the road, this car could. The rack and pinion steering gear transmits road reaction on some surfaces, but the car's response to the wishes of its driver is quite exceptionally quick and precise.

Contributing to the Minor's handling qualities is a suspension system which, using torsion bars at the front and leaf springs at the back, is firm enough to keep body roll within very small limits without any aid from anti-roll torsion bars. Lightly laden, the car has a quicker motion when driven over rough surfaces than some more softly-sprung types, a heavier passenger load softening the suspension, but the ride is flat and the springing gives effective insulation against shock as well as fatigue-free fast travel. General road-holding qualities are excellent, even though the rear axle carries no more than 41½% of the unladen weight, but on loose surfaces or occasionally at other times axle-tramp can be induced by hard acceleration in first or second gear.

A "chassis" which asks to be compared with sports cars is well matched by a power unit which, although docile, responds very willingly to a hard driver's use of the gear lever. For maximum acceleration, upward changes of gear are made at roughly 20, 30-35 and 55 m.p.h., the remote-control central gear lever being positive in action and conveniently positioned; the synchromesh on three of the four ratios is genuinely helpful, although it can be over-ridden by a driver in a real hurry. Open-road cruising in this modestly-dimensioned car at speeds around 65 m.p.h. does not seem to tire either mechanism or crew, the engine being quite well silenced. The clutch is positive almost to the point of fierceness, and the gearbox quiet under load, although less quiet on the over-run.

Rather small in size, but reasonably tolerant of broad footwear, the pedals are comfortable for most people and more suitable for feminine high-heel shoes than are some layouts. Although the clutch and footbrake are not perhaps quite as light to operate as might be expected on a small car, the brakes were well up to their job, resistant to fade but rather apt to lock the rear wheels in emergencies unless there was weight in the rear of the car. On damp mornings, the first few brake applications were apt to produce rather fierce response.

Our test being in summer conditions, we cannot make up-to-date comments

In Brief

Price £436 plus purchase tax £182 15s. 10d. equals £618 15s. 10d.

Capacity	948 c.c.
Unladen kerb weight ...	14¾ cwt.
Acceleration:	
20-40 m.p.h. in top gear ...	14.6 sec.
0-50 m.p.h. through gears	16.0 sec.
Maximum direct top gear	
gradient	1 in 13.3
Maximum speed	73.2 m.p.h.
"Maximile" speed	70.7 m.p.h.
Touring fuel consumption ...	39.5 m.p.g.

Gearing: 15.0 m.p.h. in top gear at 1,000 r.p.m.; 30.1 m.p.h. at 1,000 ft./min. piston speed.

Morris Minor 1000
Convertible de luxe

CONVENTIONAL fore-and-aft location of the 948 c.c. engine leaves plenty of spare room beneath a broad bonnet. Note that even the front shock absorbers are easily accessible.

about engine starting in really cold weather, but presume that this remains easy. Conveniently, the "choke" control of the S.U. carburetter gives a speeded tick-over without mixture enrichment during the first notches of its travel (it has a convenient twist-to-release action) and rich mixture only when pulled out rather further, but until warmed up by a short drive, the engine seemed a rather sluggish performer. Apart from the obvious economy indicated by steady-speed consumption figures such as 52 m.p.g. at 40 m.p.h. and 36½ m.p.g. at 60 m.p.h., this power unit will save money for its owner by operating without any trace of knock on intermediate-grade petrols such as retail in London at about 4s. 6d. per gallon.

For this test we were loaned a de luxe Morris Minor 1000 with the convertible body, which is an alternative to two-door

and four-door saloons of similar carrying capacity. Costing no more than the two-door saloon, and with almost every saloon-car amenity except sun visors, an interior light and a lined roof, this convertible model is exceptionally attractive value for its tax-paid price of £618 15s. 10d. When the roof is folded, it offers genuine open-car vision and ventilation, save for the continued presence of front window frames and of fixed rear windows. If the design has a limitation, it is that, with a dozen

press-stud hood fixings above and behind the windows as well as the usual two fastenings above the windscreen, and six press-studs on the neat hood bag, weatherproofness has been combined with complete folding of the roof by acceptance of the need for single-handed raising or folding away of the roof to take several minutes. In respect of almost complete freedom from rattle, this model shames the majority of larger and more expensive convertibles, although on corrugated road surfaces absence of the extra structural stiffeners which a steel-roof panel provides can be detected.

Inside the body, the Minor 1000 has a rather more functional air than is nowadays usual, the facia a comparatively flat painted-metal panel with a large circular speedometer dial incorporating a fuel contents gauge as the sole instruments, and considerable numbers of screw heads unashamedly visible and accessible. Most people find this slightly plain interior far from offensive, it being relieved by pile carpets on the floor and by leather-upholstered seats. The individual seats (between which a pull-up handbrake is mounted very conveniently) have transverse rubber straps beneath their cushioning, and provide quite good comfort. Only the driving seat is adjustable, and that clumsily over a very limited range, but alternative mounting points on the floor allow for the passenger seat and/or the whole range of driving-seat adjustment being semi-permanently set back a short distance if legroom in the front is more valuable than rear-seat roominess.

Whilst the use of a sloping tail does not allow for quite such vast luggage capacity as exists in some more square-cut modern bodies, this car has a very useful luggage locker, with its floor completely flat and the spare wheel slid onto a separate shelf which can also accommodate tools and some parcels. Inside the luggage locker, so that it cannot be reached without a key, there is a strap fastening which can be undone to let the rear-seat backrest fold forwards or be removed, so that a long or bulky load can extend from the luggage locker into the body, the extreme of carrying capacity being obtained when the front passenger seat also is folded and tipped forward against the facia.

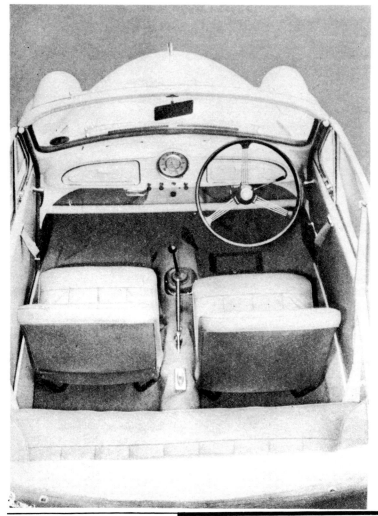

DOWNWARD view into the convertible body shows the positive-action central gear lever and pull-up handbrake between individual front seats, and the parcel shelf below a facia which also has two glove boxes flanking the speedometer/fuel gauge dial.

FOLDING with the weatherproof hood, the rear window has a large area of clear plastic. The spare wheel is stowed separately from the luggage, capacity for which can be increased by folding forward or removing the rear seat backrest.

cover would be a full-length tonneau cover so that the seats could be protected against unexpected showers when the car is parked with its hood down.

Whilst the Morris Minor 1000 may now lack the appeal of novelty, its continued availability in de Luxe convertible form at a price of only £436 (plus purchase tax amounting to £182 15s. 10d. in Britain) makes it astonishingly good value for money. Extended development of what was in the first place a brilliantly clever design has produced a car in which low-cost motoring can be exceptionally enjoyable.

Amenities which are expected in a saloon and retained in this inexpensive Convertible include wind-down windows supplemented by hinged triangular ventilators on the front doors. The rear quarter windows are fixed, but the hood incorporates a flexible and truly transparent rear window of quite large size through which a big rear-view mirror provides good vision. There is also a simple heating system included in the de luxe specification, the water tap being on the engine so that the heater must be controlled mainly by the rheostat which varies its fan speed, or by means of a push-pull control on the facia which lets the heater circulate air from inside the car or admit air from in-

takes beneath the front mudguards. A relic of the V-screen which preceded the curved glass now used is evident in the windscreen-wiper layout, which ignores a large area at the centre of the glass.

As an open car, we found the Minor Convertible extremely attractive, whether it was being used in London's congested streets, to explore country lanes, or for fast main-road travel. There is a circulation of air behind the curved windscreen which produces a forward draught beneath and around the tubular-framed front seats, but mile-a-minute cruising with the car open hardly disturbs the hair of a bare-headed driver. As with almost any open car, a sensible supplement to the hood

The World Copyright of this article and illustrations is strictly reserved   © Temple Press Limited, 1959

Specification

Engine

Cylinders	4
Bore	62.93 mm.
Stroke	76.2 mm.
Cubic capacity	948 c.c.
Piston area	19.3 sq. in.
Valves	In-line o.h.v. (pushrods)
Compression ratio	8.3/1 (optional 7.2/1)
Carburetter	S.U. inclined type H2
Fuel pump	S.U. electrical
Ignition timing control	Centrifugal and vacuum
Oil filter	Full-flow Tecalemit 2A693 or Purolator 2A789
Max. power (gross)	37 b.h.p. (35 b.h.p. net)

(Low compression engine gives 3 b.h.p. less power output)

at	4,800 r.p.m.
Piston speed at max. b.h.p.	2,400 ft./min.

Transmission

Clutch	Borg & Beck 6¼ in. single dry plate
Top gear (s/m)	4.555
3rd gear (s/m)	6.425
2nd gear (s/m)	10.802
1st gear	16.507
Reverse	21.221
Propeller shaft	Hardy Spicer open
Final drive	9/41 hypoid bevel
Top gear m.p.h. at 1,000 r.p.m.	15.0
Top gear m.p.h. at 1,000 ft./min. piston speed	30.1

Chassis

Brakes	Lockheed hydraulic, 2 l.s. front
Brake drum internal diameter	7 in.
Friction lining area	63.8 sq. in.
Suspension:	
Front	Independent by torsion bars and transverse wishbones
Rear	Semi-elliptic leaf springs
Shock absorbers	Armstrong lever-arm hydraulic
Steering gear	Rack and pinion
Tyres	Dunlop tubeless, 5.00—14

Coachwork and Equipment

Starting handle	Yes
Battery mounting	On scuttle behind engine
Jack	Bipod screw type, operated by starting handle
Jacking points	2 external sockets under body sides

Standard tool kit: Jack, combined wheelbrace and starting handle, grease gun, tyre pump, sparking plug spanner, hub cover removal key, tyre valve key, distributor feeler and screwdriver, axle drain plug key.

Exterior lights:	2 headlamps, 2 sidelamps, 2 stop/tail lamps, number plate lamp.
Number of electrical fuses	2
Direction indicators:	Semaphore type, self cancelling (flashers on export models).
Windscreen wipers	Electrical two-blade, self-parking
Windscreen washers	None
Sun visors	None on Convertible
Instruments:	Speedometer with non-decimal total distance recorder, fuel contents gauge.
Warning lights:	Dynamo charge, oil pressure, direction indicators, headlamp main beam.

Locks:

With ignition key	Ignition switch, driver's door, luggage locker
With other keys	None
Glove lockers	2 on facia with non-locking lids.
Map pockets	None
Parcel shelves:	Full-width shelf below facia, shallow hood-well behind rear seat can be used for parcels when car is closed.
Ashtrays	One below facia
Cigar lighters	None
Interior lights	None (except internal lighting of instruments)
Interior heater	Fresh air type, with screen de-misters
Extras available	Radio
Upholstery material	Leather on wearing surfaces, and matching leathercloth
Floor covering	Pile carpets over felt
Exterior colours standardized	6
Alternative body styles:	Convertible without de luxe equipment, 2-door and 4-door standard and de luxe saloons, "Traveller" 2-door Utility.

Maintenance

Sump (including filter)	7 pints, S.A.E.30 (below freezing, S.A.E.20)
Gearbox	2¼ pints, S.A.E.30
Rear axle	1½ pints, S.A.E. 90 hypoid gear oil
Steering gear lubricant	S.A.E. 90 hypoid gear oil
Cooling system capacity	9¾ pints (2 drain taps)

Chassis lubrication: By grease gun every 1,000 miles to 10 points

Ignition timing	T.d.c. static
Contact-breaker gap	0.014-0.016 in.
Sparking plug type	Champion N5, 14 mm., ⅞-in. reach
Sparking plug gap	0.025 in.

Valve timing:	Inlet opens 5° before t.d.c. and closes 45° after b.d.c.; exhaust opens 40° before b.d.c. and closes 10° after t.d.c.
Tappet clearances (cold)	Inlet and exhaust 0.012 in.
Front wheel toe-in	⅛ in. at rims
Camber angle	1°
Castor angle	3°
Steering swivel pin inclination	7½°
Tyre pressures:	
Front	22 lb.
Rear	22-24 lb. according to load
Brake fluid	Lockheed, or to S.A.E. Spec. 70R1
Battery	Lucas 12-volt, 43 amp. hr.

Miscellaneous: Top up carburetter dashpot with S.A.E. 20 engine oil every 1,000 miles

The Motor Road Test No: 23/59

Make: Morris   **Type:** Minor 1000 Convertible de Luxe

Makers: Morris Motors Ltd., Cowley, Oxford.

Test Data

World copyright reserved ; no unauthorized reproduction in whole or in part.

CONDITIONS: *Weather Warm and dry with strong diagonal wind. (Temperature 63°-67°F., Barometer 29.7 in. Hg.) Surface: Dry tarred Macadam. Fuel: Intermediate-grade pump petrols (approx. 90 Research Method Octane Rating).*

INSTRUMENTS
Speedometer at 30 m.p.h. .. .. Accurate
Speedometer at 60 m.p.h. .. .. 3% fast
Distance recorder .. .. .. 2% fast

WEIGHT
Kerb weight (unladen, but with oil, water and
fuel for approx. 50 miles) .. 14¾ cwt.
Front/rear distribution of kerb weight 58½/41½
Weight laden as tested .. .. .. 18½ cwt.

MAXIMUM SPEEDS
Flying Quarter Mile
Mean of four opposite runs .. .. 73.2 m.p.h.
Best one-way time equals .. .. 75.3 m.p.h.

"Maximile" Speed. (Timed quarter mile after one mile accelerating from rest.)
Mean of four opposite runs .. .. 70.7 m.p.h.
Best one-way time equals .. .. 73.2 m.p.h.

Speed in gears
Max. speed in 3rd gear .. .. 62 m.p.h.
Max. speed in 2nd gear .. .. 38 m.p.h.
Max. speed in 1st gear .. .. 25 m.p.h.

FUEL CONSUMPTION
57.0 m.p.g. at constant 30 m.p.h. on level.
52.0 m.p.g. at constant 40 m.p.h. on level.
42.5 m.p.g. at constant 50 m.p.h. on level.
36.5 m.p.g. at constant 60 m.p.h. on level.

Overall Fuel Consumption for 1,188 miles, 31.4 gallons, equals 37.8 m.p.g. (7.5 litres/100 km.)

Touring Fuel Consumption (m.p.g. at steady speed midway between 30 m.p.h. and maximum, less 5% allowance for acceleration). 39.5 m.p.g.
Fuel tank capacity (maker's figure) 6½ gallons

STEERING
Turning circle between kerbs:
Left .. .. 29¾ feet
Right .. .. 32¼ feet
Turns of steering wheel from lock to lock 2⅓

BRAKES from 30 m.p.h.
0.96g retardation (equivalent to 31¼ ft. stopping distance) with 125 lb. pedal pressure
0.77g retardation (equivalent to 39 ft. stopping distance) with 100 lb. pedal pressure
0.63g retardation (equivalent to 48 ft. stopping distance) with 75 lb. pedal pressure
0.40g retardation (equivalent to 75 ft. stopping distance) with 50 lb. pedal pressure
0.16g retardation (equivalent to 188 ft. stopping distance) with 25 lb. pedal pressure

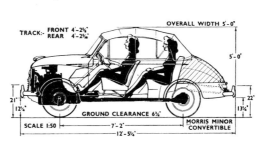

TRACK:- FRONT 4'-2⅛"
REAR 4'-2⁵⁄₁₆"
OVERALL WIDTH 5'-0"
5'-0"
21" 12¾" GROUND CLEARANCE 6¼" 22" 13¼"
SCALE 1:50
7'-2"
12'-5¼"
MORRIS MINOR CONVERTIBLE

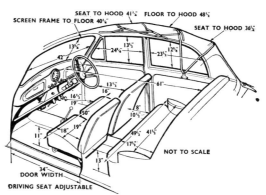

SEAT TO HOOD 41½"   FLOOR TO HOOD 48½"
SCREEN FRAME TO FLOOR 40¼"
SEAT TO HOOD 36¼"
13¾"   13½"   12¾"
42"   24¼"   23½"
13½"   6'1"
16¼"   16"
19"
50"   8"
10½"
18"   19"   49½"   41¾"
11"   17¾"
NOT TO SCALE
13"   DRIVING SEAT ADJUSTABLE
34" DOOR WIDTH

ACCELERATION TIMES from standstill		ACCELERATION TIMES on upper ratios		
			Top gear	3rd gear
0-30 m.p.h.	6.2 sec.	10-30 m.p.h.	13.7 sec.	8.8 sec.
0-40 m.p.h.	10.5 sec.	20-40 m.p.h.	14.6 sec.	9.4 sec.
0-50 m.p.h.	16.0 sec.	30-50 m.p.h.	15.6 sec.	11.0 sec.
0-60 m.p.h.	25.9 sec.	40-60 m.p.h.	20.0 sec.	—
Standing quarter mile ..	23.4 sec.			

HILL CLIMBING at sustained steady speeds
Max. gradient on top gear .. .. 1 in 13.3 (Tapley 165 lb./ton)
Max. gradient on 3rd gear .. .. 1 in 8.4 (Tapley 265 lb./ton)
Max. gradient on 2nd gear .. .. 1 in 5.3 (Tapley 415 lb./ton)

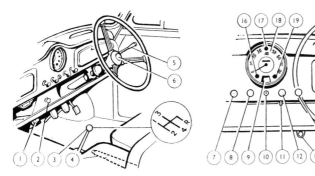

1, Headlamp dip switch. 2, Heater fan control. 3, Gear lever. 4, Handbrake. 5, Direction indicator switch and warning light. 6, Horn button. 7, Choke control. 8, Windscreen wipers switch. 9, Fuel contents gauge. 10, Ignition switch. 11, Panel light switch. 12, Lights switch. 13, Heater air inlet control. 14, Starter. 15, Bonnet catch release. 16, Oil pressure warning light. 17, Headlamp main beam indicator. 18, Speedometer and distance recorder. 19, Dynamo charge warning light.

c16

Autocar road test 1973

Morris Minor 1000 de luxe 1,098 c.c.

BACK in 1960, when we carried out our full test of a Morris Minor 1000, it would have needed a competent *clairvoyant* to predict that four years later the car would still be in production and selling well. So it is, however, and the numerous changes introduced in the meantime include the fourth different engine since the Minor was first announced in 1948. Many less prominent improvements also have been incorporated in the latest model.

With the changeover to a 1,098 c.c. engine, the Minor falls into line with all the B.M.C. range using the A-series power unit, except for the Minis; and both bore and stroke are increased to give the 150 c.c. extra swept volume. A small rise in compression ratio to 8.5 to 1 (formerly 8.3) still allows the engine to run satisfactorily on mixture grade fuel. At 48 b.h.p. (net) maximum power is up by 30 per cent, and the curve peaks at 5,100 r.p.m. instead of at 4,750 r.p.m.

Even to those familiar with the previous model, the extra liveliness expected from such a major step-up in power output does not feel particularly marked. Yet the linear

comparisons reproduced on this page show that the Minor's latest engine change puts it on a competitive footing with its more modern rivals, and reference to the previous road test shows, for example, a reduction of nearly 6sec, in the standstill to 60 m.p.h. acceleration time.

A very welcome innovation is that the new Minor is also somewhat higher geared, with a 4-22 axle in place of 4-55 to 1, and this may explain why the maximum speeds of

PRICES		£	s	d
Four-door de luxe saloon		474	10	0
Purchase Tax		99	8	4
	Total (in G.B.)	573	18	4
Extras (inc. P.T.)				
Smiths radio (push button)		33	0	0
Safety belts (each)*		3	5	0
*As from 4 May				

How the Morris Minor 1000 compares:

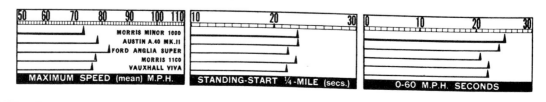

MORRIS MINOR 1000
AUSTIN A.40 MK.II
FORD ANGLIA SUPER
MORRIS 1100
VAUXHALL VIVA

MAXIMUM SPEED (mean) M.P.H.   STANDING-START ¼-MILE (secs.)   0-60 M.P.H. SECONDS

Autocar road test · No. 1973

Make · MORRIS   Type · Minor 1000 (1,098 c.c.)
(Front engine, rear-wheel drive)

Manufacturer : Morris Motors Ltd., Cowley, Oxford

Test Conditions
Weather...... Dry, overcast, with 10-15 m.p.h. wind
Temperature .... 2 deg. C. (36 deg. F.)
Barometer.................................... 29·4in. Hg.
Dry concrete and asphalt surfaces.

Weight
Kerb weight (with oil, water and half-full fuel tank)
15·25cwt (1,708lb-775kg)
Front-rear distribution, per cent F, 57·4; R, 42·6
Laden as tested......... 18·25cwt (2,044lb-927kg)

Turning Circles
Between kerbs .... L, 32ft 5in.; R, 33ft 5in.
Between walls .... L, 33ft 11in.; R, 34ft 11in.
Turns of steering wheel lock to lock .... 2·5

FUEL AND OIL CONSUMPTION

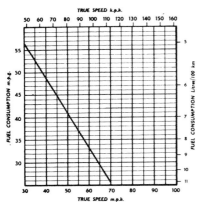

FUEL .... Mixture grade
(92–94 octane RM)
Test Distance........................ 1,173 miles
Overall Consumption .... 31·2 m.p.g.
(9·1 litres/100 km.)
Estimated Consumption (DIN) 33·8 m.p.g.
(8·4 litres/100 km.)
OIL: SAE 10/30...... Consumption 7,500 m.p.g.

MAXIMUM SPEEDS AND ACCELERATION TIMES

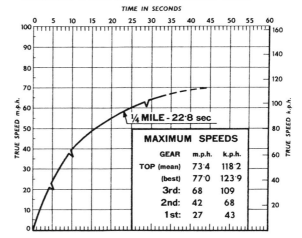

¼ MILE - 22·8 sec

MAXIMUM SPEEDS		
GEAR	m.p.h.	k.p.h.
TOP (mean)	73·4	118·2
(best)	77·0	123·9
3rd:	68	109
2nd:	42	68
1st:	27	43

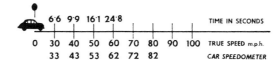

					TIME IN SECONDS
6·6	9·9	16·1	24·8		
0	30 40 50 60 70 80 90 100				TRUE SPEED m.p.h.
	33 43 53 62 72 82				CAR SPEEDOMETER

Speed range, overall gear ratios and time in seconds

m.p.h.	Top (4·22)	Third (5·96)	Second (10·07)	First (15·52)
10—30	—	9·0	5·8	—
20—40	13·6	9·2	6·4	—
30—50	16·3	11·0	—	—
40—60	21·9	15·3	—	—

BRAKES	Pedal Load	Retardation	Equiv. distance
(from 30 m.p.h.	25lb	0·16g	188ft
in neutral)	50lb	0·40g	75ft
	75lb	0·68g	44ft
	100lb	0·95g	31·7ft
Handbrake		0·20g	150ft

CLUTCH   Pedal load and travel—35lb and 4in.

HILL CLIMBING AT STEADY SPEEDS

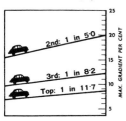

2nd: 1 in 5·0
3rd: 1 in 8·2
Top: 1 in 11·7

GEAR PULL (lb per ton)	Top	Third	Second
	190	270	440

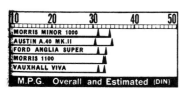

10	20	30	40	50
MORRIS MINOR 1000				
AUSTIN A.40 MK.II				
FORD ANGLIA SUPER				
MORRIS 1100				
VAUXHALL VIVA				

M.P.G. Overall and Estimated (DIN)

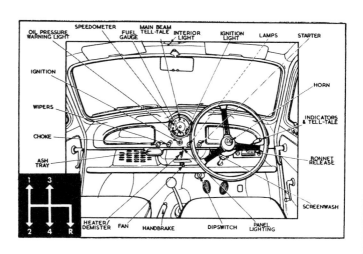

AUTOCAR, 8 May 1964

Morris
Minor 1000
4-door . . .

Rather loose-fitting carpets cover the floor, and there is washable plastic for the roof lining. The steering-wheel is deeply dished for accident safety, and has the button for the rather meek horn in its boss. The indicator switch is self-cancelling, with a green light at the end of its stem

73·4 (mean) and 77 m.p.h. (best, with following wind) are little better than those of the 948 c.c. car. The new model holds the higher speeds with less effort, and is capable of 70 m.p.h. even with a slight head wind. It is also under less strain when driven at sustained full throttle on a motorway, engine revs at 70 m.p.h. being down from 4,600 to 4,320 r.p.m.

With gradient in the car's favour, speed may build up to appreciably more than 80 m.p.h., but this is well within the safe range of the engine. There is still considerable engine roar, mingled with a fair amount of wind and tyre noise at these speeds, and most Minor 1000 drivers probably would hold nearer 60 m.p.h. for prolonged cruising.

As well as being kinder to the machinery, this rate of progress is also much better for the pocket; by holding a steady 60 m.p.h. one can cover eight more miles on a gallon of petrol than at 70 m.p.h. Not unnaturally, extra performance cost more in petrol, and the overall consumption of 31·2 m.p.g. is 3·5 lower than was recorded with the previous model. The figure includes a fair proportion of town running, but only one return trip on M1. Owners who drive quietly will still obtain an easy 35 m.p.g. and the consumption figures at constant speeds are appreciably better up to 50 m.p.h. than with the previous lower-geared Minor. The 6¼-gallon tank just allows a range of 200 miles.

Ranking with such metal as Jaguar and Rolls-Royce, the Morris Minor 1000 is one of the last cars to retain a separate starter control divorced from the ignition switch; it works by direct cable to a large relay switch on the bulkhead. Renowned for reliability and simplicity, the Minor is also a ready starter. The engine pulls without hesitation, and the mixture control can be pressed home by the time the car is in top gear.

A larger clutch is now used to absorb the extra power, and it has a particularly easy and light pedal action which even a learner will quickly master. Clutch drag developed with the test car, corrected by an easy adjustment of its linkage. More serious was the "loss" of second and third gears some days after the performance figures had been recorded. In our experience these faults are not typical of a basically good and simple transmission.

Although the transmission gears were quiet, the propeller shaft was clearly out of balance and excited some vibration and drumming in the body at certain speeds. Some occa-

sional loud and strange noises from below when the car rode a big bump—even small bumps when there were three or four people aboard—were traced to the "head" of a Jubilee clip used as a balance weight round the propeller shaft tube fouling the handbrake cable.

The gearbox, in particular, is first-class, and the remote control lever has a light action. A diagram of the gate layout embossed in the gear lever knob is uncomfortable to the hand, and scarcely seems necessary for such a straightforward change. Baulk-ring synchromesh on the three upper gears has solved the old difficulty of gear crunch, when drivers took advantage of the rapid movement possible, particularly between first and second. Although having no synchromesh, first gear is scarcely ever difficult to engage with the car at rest—once a familiar grouse with the Minor 1000. If this does happen, momentary release of the clutch and a second try solves the problem. As there is a very good pick-up from a walking pace in second gear a change down to first on the move is very rarely needed, but if it should be necessary, a quick double-declutch usually provides a silent engagement.

Even with the slightly higher gearing, and maximum engine torque at 2,500 r.p.m. as before, there is smooth and willing response to the throttle from down to about 15 m.p.h. in top gear, but the ratios encourage the driver to use the gearbox freely. Third gear provides a useful span of acceleration from as low as 10 m.p.h. right through to 60 m.p.h., with a rather noisy maximum of 68 m.p.h. if taken to the limit. Second gear, as well as being effec-

The spare wheel tucks away into its own compartment, with space for tools, under the boot floor

AUTOCAR, 8 May 1964
579

Overriders identify the de luxe model. As the new 1,098 c.c. version is still called the Minor 1000, car spotters must rely on the amber winking indicators to distinguish it from earlier models. Only the driver's door can be locked with a key

tively higher by use of the 4.22 axle, has its ratio raised as well, allowing a maximum speed of about 42 m.p.h., against only 34 m.p.h. with the predecessor.

Since its original introduction, the Morris Minor has always featured excellent steering as one of its foremost qualities and, with slight reservation, this still applies. Wheel tremor, which used to be felt through the steering on bad roads, has been reduced to a minimum, and although the control seems now a shade less positive than before, it is still among the best of current production cars for the combination of accuracy and lightness. In strong crosswinds on M1, only the tiniest corrections are needed to keep exactly to a straight course. A reasonably compact turning circle of 33ft (between kerbs), and steering which can be turned easily with the car scarcely moving, yet takes only 2½ turns lock to lock, all help to ease the task of manœuvring and parking in cramped quarters.

Improved Suspension

Minor suspension was a major revelation of simplicity for an independent front layout when it first came on the scene, with its use of longitudinal torsion bars and damper arms to form the top links. But with advances in the understanding of suspension behaviour and technology, average standards of ride comfort have progressed during the decade since that time. Improved dampers and bumpstops have cured the once characteristic rebound rattle from the front suspension over severe bumps, but the ride is firm and lively for 1964. Small surface irregularities are not picked up too badly, but a major hump creates quite a lurch.

On poorly surfaced corners axle hop causes the back end to run wide, and calls for snappy correction in the wet, when tyre adhesion is poor. On smoother, dry roads the car behaves much better, and one recalls that the good road manners and easy control of the Minor as much as anything have been responsible for the model's prolonged popularity. Slight understeer, understandable considering more than 57 per cent of the total weight is carried by the front wheels, results in predictable handling which reassures inexperienced drivers. In extreme conditions there is sufficient weight transfer to allow the inside rear wheel to spin, but this is no longer accompanied by the axle tramp which was an embarrassment with earlier Minors.

A paper element air cleaner, identical with that of the Morris 1100, is now fitted, and can be arranged to collect cool air in summer, or hot air from around the exhaust manifold for winter running. For all its power increases over the years, the engine still looks small and compact in the spacious compartment

An all-drum braking system is retained, but at the front both diameter and lining width have been increased, stepping up the total swept area from 54 to 74 sq. in. A firm push on the pedal is needed for hard braking, but brings powerful response without skidding and a reassuring 0·95g stop to take care of emergencies. Free travel of the pedal did not increase, and no fade occurred during testing. Pulled on really hard, the handbrake is quite efficient, and just held the car on 1-in-3; but it is of limited value as an emergency stand-by if the main system should fail, as only 0·2g retardation can be obtained before one rear wheel locks. In other words, it would need about 150ft to stop from 30 m.p.h. The lever is placed conveniently between the seats.

Among many detail changes of decor, completely different seat trim is noticed, using Vynair and leathercloth, as on early Morris 1100s. Standard Minors have all-leathercloth seats. The upholstery is pretty firm, and there is little lateral support to hold one in place on corners, these being essentially seats that one sits "on" rather than "sinking into". The driving position is a fair compromise, and for tall drivers alternative mounting holes allow the seat to be repositioned 1in. farther back. Intrusion of the wheel arch restricts toeboard width on each side, and causes the pedals to be offset to the left; but there is still room for the driver's left foot to rest beside the clutch pedal. Even in this four-door model both front seats tilt forward, allowing oddments to be stowed underneath them.

The heater unit, similar to that now fitted to the Minis, collects air from the front of the car, beside the radiator,

and has three positions—off, cold, and hot. Variation of the air flow is not possible. A single-speed and reasonably quiet fan is fitted; there is no rheostat control as there was on the previous model. A narrow jet of warm air is delivered, which travels straight down the centre of the car to the rear compartment, making this one of the few where those in the back really do as well in this respect as those in front. In fact one might well suffer from cold feet (in the direct sense) in front. As well as the heater, the de luxe specification includes the different seat trim already mentioned, bumper overriders front and rear, and a sun visor for the passenger—additions which collectively add some £28 to the total cost of the four-door model, and £24 to the two-door version. The heater is not available as an extra for the standard model.

Still of the old pattern incorporating separate bulbs, the headlamps give ample range and spread for the full performance to be used at night. There is a foot dipswitch, but no flasher. A big improvement has been made in the windscreen wipers, of which the pivots are now both offset to the right, and sweep in unison instead of the previous arrangement designed for the original divided windscreen. A large area of the glass is covered by arcs with a good overlap in the middle; and a simple and effective Wingard screen washer is fitted on all models.

Huge amber flashers at each end have taken the place of the previous ones with twin filament bulbs; they are certainly businesslike and meant to be seen. There is no reversing lamp. Opening either of the front doors lights the roof lamp.

Although the bonnet support is self-fixing, to secure the boot lid a separate stay still has to be fixed in position—an operation needing two free hands. The stay rod also tended to fall out of its rubber socket when the boot lid was slammed, and had gouged the wooden floor of the compartment.

After releasing a Lift-the-Dot fastener inside the boot the rear seat squab pushes forward, to allow the luggage space to extend right into the back of the car for carrying long or awkwardly shaped loads. From personal experience of Minors we know this to be very useful. As well as a wide parcels tray in front, there are two small lockers in the facia, but they no longer have lids, and tend to eject their contents on to one's legs during a fast getaway. A good Smiths push-button radio on the test car was within easy reach of the driver, and its speaker accepted sufficient volume to be heard well at speed.

An aspect, that dates the Minor design is the rather restricted visibility confined by broad screen pillars and what now seems rather high scuttle. The central mounting of the large speedometer dial, where it is sometimes obscured by the driver's left hand on the wheel, is a production economy for left- or right-hand drive markets, and is inferior to the facia layout of the original Series MM Minor.

In other directions the car has advanced considerably and kept abreast of overall progress. Not least of its improvements is the extension from 1,000 to 3,000 miles between periodic attention to its 11 grease points. Multigrade oil in the engine needs to be changed only at 6,000-mile intervals.

Specification: Morris Minor 1000 de luxe

PERFORMANCE DATA

Top gear m.p.h. per 1,000 r.p.m.	16·2
Mean piston speed at max. power	2,810ft/min.
Engine revs. at mean max. speed	4,530 r.p.m.
B.h.p. per ton laden	52·6

▼ *Scale: 0·3in. to 1ft. Cushions uncompressed.*

ENGINE

Cylinders	...	4-in-line, water-cooled
Bore	...	64·6mm (2·54in.)
Stroke	...	83·7mm (3·30in.)
Displacement	...	1,098 c.c. (67 cu in.)
Valve gear	...	Overhead, pushrods and rockers
Compression ratio	8·5-to-1; optional 7·5 to 1	
Carburettor	...	Single S.U. HS2 semi-down-draught
Fuel pump	...	S.U. electric
Oil filter	...	Purolator or Tecalemit full-flow, replaceable element
Max. power	...	48 b.h.p. (net) at 5,100 r.p.m.
Max. torque	...	60 lb. ft at 2,500 r.p.m.

TRANSMISSION

Clutch	...	Borg and Beck, single dry-plate, 7·25in. dia.
Gearbox	...	Four-speed, synchromesh on 2nd, 3rd and Top, central floor change
Ratios	...	Top 1·0, Third 1·41, Second 2·55, First 3·68, Reverse 4·66
Final drive	...	Hypoid, 4·22 to 1

CHASSIS

Construction	...	Integral with steel body

SUSPENSION

Front	...	Independent, wishbones, torsion bars, lever-arm dampers forming top links of suspension
Rear	...	Half-elliptic leaf springs, lever-arm dampers
Steering	...	Rack-and-pinion
Wheel dia.	...	17in.

BRAKES

Type	...	Lockheed hydraulic; drums, no servo
Dimensions	...	F, 8in. dia. drums, 1·47in. wide shoes. R, 7in. dia drums, 1·22in. wide shoes
Swept area	...	F, 74 sq. in.; R, 53·7 sq. in. Total: 127·7 sq. in (140 sq. in. per ton laden)

WHEELS

Type	...	Pressed steel disc, 4-stud fixing, 3·5in. wide rim
Tyres	...	Dunlop C41 tubeless 5.00—14in.

EQUIPMENT

Battery	...	12-volt 43-amp. hr.
Headlamps	...	Lucas (separate bulbs) 50-40-watt
Reversing lamp	...	None
Electric fuses	...	2
Screen wipers	...	Two-blade, single-speed, self-parking
Screen washer	...	Standard on de luxe models
Interior heater	...	Standard on de luxe models
Safety belts	...	Extra, anchorages provided
Interior trim	...	Vynair and leathercloth
Floor covering	...	Pile carpet
Starting handle	...	Standard
Jack	...	Screw type
Jacking points	...	One on each side of body
Other bodies	...	Estate car, two-door saloon and tourer

MAINTENANCE

Fuel tank	...	6·5 Imp. gallons (no reserve)
Cooling system	...	9·75 pints (including heater)
Engine sump	...	6·5 pints SAE 10/30 multigrade. Change oil every 6,000 miles; change filter element every 6,000 miles
Gearbox	...	2·25 pints multigrade SAE 10/30. No change recommended with multigrade
Final drive	...	1·5 pints SAE 90. No change recommended
Grease	...	11 points every 3,000 miles
Tyre pressures	...	F, 22; R, 22 p.s.i. (normal driving); F,22; R, 24 p.s.i. (full load)

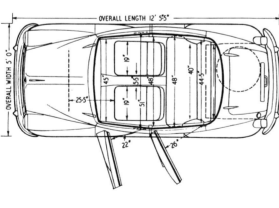

OVERALL LENGTH 12' 5⋅5"
OVERALL WIDTH 5' 0"

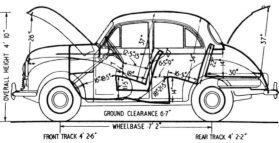

OVERALL HEIGHT 4' 10"
GROUND CLEARANCE 6·7"
WHEELBASE 7' 2"
FRONT TRACK 4' 2·6"   REAR TRACK 4' 2·2"

OWNER'S VIEW

Ray Newell interviews Pat Carlsson, formerly Pat Moss, who successfully rallied Morris Minors in International competitions. Pat and her family live in Buckinghamshire.

R.N. When did you first become interested in Morris Minors?
P.C. When I bought my first car which was a sidevalve model.
R.N. When was that?
P.C. 1951.
R.N. What other Morris Minors have you owned?
P.C. Except for my present car, none, though I drove and borrowed factory ones and a privately owned convertible. Then of course there was "Grannie" the saloon I rallied. Her registration number was NMO 933. My brother, Stirling, owned an early M.M. — he added a Derrington conversion to improve its performance.
R.N. When did you buy the Morris Minor you own now?
P.C. Three years ago.
R.N. What model is it?
P.C. It's a green 1966 Morris 1000 convertible.
R.N. What sort of condition was it in when you bought it?
P.C. It was a runner, in fairly good condition — not too much rust but the brakes had had it and the interior was a bit tatty.
R.N. What repairs/renovations have you had done to it?

P.C. The engine and gearbox have been overhauled. It's had two new wings, been rustproofed and completely resprayed. I've bought some new carpets and intend to replace some of the interior trim later. I'm also having all electrical items checked.
R.N. Would it have been economic to have bought a car in better of worse condition than yours initially?
P.C. Not at the price we paid! After all, convertibles *are* hard to find.
R.N. Have you experienced any difficulty in obtaining any parts?
P.C. Not yet, the carpet and the wings were easy to get and they were cheap.
R.N. Is your car in everyday use yet?
P.C. Not really. I've driven it a few times but it will be in use more in the summer months.
R.N. How practical do you think it will be?
P.C. O.K. in Summer, but I hope the heater will be better than the ones in the Morris Minors I've had before!
R.N. What sort of handling and performance does the car have?
P.C. It's a very good runner and its road holding is fair. The brakes leave something to be desired and there is some axle tramp if it is cornered fast.
R.N. What successes did you have when you rallied Morris Minors in International competition?
P.C. My co-driver Anne Wisdom (now Anne Riley) and I competed with "Grannie" NMO 933 in all the major International rallies except the Alpine. "Grannie" finished them all except for the Monte. I hit a concrete post in a snowdrift! "Grannie's" radiator was just not up to it. Perhaps the best result was fourth place overall in the R.A.C. Rally in 1958 — the weather was apalling — heavy snow and hard packed ice. "Grannie" was first in the 1000cc touring car class and we took the Ladies Cup.
R.N. Are you a member of a

Morris Minor Car Club?
P.C. No, I didn't know there was one until you told me.
R.N. Is there a Morris Minor specialist whom you have found particularly useful?
P.C. No. So far I've not had cause to need one.
R.N. How would you sum up the enjoyment you get from your Morris Minor?
P.C. In my case its largely still to come. I hope lots of sun and fresh air — the joys of open top motoring.
R.N. What advice would you give to the potential buyer of a Morris Minor?
P.C. If it's a very good, reliable and economical little car you're looking for, then the Morris Minor is for you.

Ray Newell interviews Jim Funnell, a Morris Minor enthusiast of many years standing. Jim owns nine Morris Minors, races a 'Morris Minor Special' and runs his own business, restoring, servicing and repairing Morris Minors at Houghton on the Hill, Leicestershire.

R.N. When did you first become interested in Morris Minors?
J.F. In 1966 when I bought my first car, a 1955 Series II 4 door saloon.
R.N. What other Morris Minors do you own?
J.F. As well as my first car, which I still have, I have two Series II cars and three Morris 1000s which are running, two possible restoration vehicles and my 'Morris Minor Special' racing car.
R.N. Which car do you use most?
J.F. The first car I bought is the one I use most. When I bought it, it had 86,000 miles on the clock. Over the years I reckon its done at least 250,000 miles. I still tax it and run it but its getting ready for another rebuild.
R.N. What sort of condition was it in when you bought it?
J.F. It was in average condition considering the mileage it had

done. The interior was good but it was showing signs of rusting in the usual places — around the headlights, down the side of the wings next to the door, and along the bottom of the doors. The underside was a bit weak in places.

R.N. What repairs/renovations and modifications did you carry out on the car?

J.F. I decided to do the car up in stages. I started with the underside and, working on each side individually, I strengthened it by using my own repair sections. Gradually I worked my way round the car repairing and replacing damaged or weak panels until all the bodywork was complete.

My interest at that time was in increasing the performance. The original 803cc engine and gearbox did not provide the speed and acceleration I wanted so I began the process of modifying the car to my individual tastes. In 1967 I started with the brakes. I fitted Riley 1.5 front brakes with AM4 brake linings and a Servo. The rear brakes remained standard except for aluminium brake drums. Brakes complete I moved on to the suspension.

Here I hoped to improve handling by lowering the front suspension and introducing about 1½° negative camber. This done I fitted a Riley 1.5 anti-roll bar, Armstrong shock absorbers and some reinforced bump stop rubbers. In order to lower the rear of the car and to reduce axle tramp, the rear leaf springs were rearranged. The bottom two leaves were interchanged with the top two on each spring and then clamped together in their new position by steel clamps. Special Aeon bump stop rubbers were then fitted along with Armstrong shock absorbers. The net result was to lower the car by half an inch. Finally the wheels and tyres were changed. Out went 14 inch wheels in came 5½ Jx13 with 165x13 tyres. This completed the suspension modifications and road

holding was dramatically improved.

All that remained was to fit the power block. For this a MkIII 1098cc Sprite engine was chosen and in 1968 a brand new short engine was bought from British Leyland. This was used in conjunction with a MkIV Sprite gearbox and over the years a variety of differential ratios have been used, including Morris 1000, Wolseley 1500 and Riley 1.5.

Features of the engine include the following: fully balanced and lightened cast iron flywheel; B.M.C. 731 camshaft; Duplex timing gears; specially machined 1275 Cooper S valves; Janspeed exhaust manifold; 1½ inch S.U. Carbs; a Mini Cooper's distributor and a front-mounted oil cooler.

The final personal touch was the addition of a sunshine roof — courtesy of a Volkswagen Beetle — and it fitted like a dream. When finished, the car drove and handled magnificently and it still gives me great pleasure to drive.

R.N. Would you have been better off buying a Morris Minor in better or worse condition to start with?

J.F. Not at that time. Anyway it was all I could afford.

R.N. Have you ever experienced any difficulty in getting parts for your cars?

J.F. Not really.

R.N. How practical is your car to run? Are your running costs high?

J.F. It's very practical. I use it to tow my Special to the race circuits. It's cheap to run and I have no problems with it.

R.N. Have you entered any of your cars in Concours competitions or the like?

J.F. I have exhibited one of my Series II cars which is in very good original condition. It's never won anything but I don't take that sort of thing very seriously.

R.N. Tell me a bit about your "Morris Minor Special".

J.F. Well it started out as a modified steel-bodied Series II Morris Minor but over the years it's developed into something quite different. While it retains the

Morris Minor shape it's now a G.R.P. shell with a tubular aluminium frame. It's powered by a Ford Cosworth B.D.A. 1300 engine.

R.N. How successful has it been in competition?

J.F. In the 1981 season I had three class wins and numerous placings in the twenty two races I competed in. I'm building a new car for the 1982/83 seasons and intend to keep the Morris Minor shape.

R.N. Are you a member of a Morris Minor Car Club?

J.F. Yes, I'm a member of the Morris Minor Owners Club.

R.N. What sort of things does the club provide for its members?

J.F. The most important thing, in my view, that the club does, is to bring together Morris Minor Owners. The club does provide a number of services like spares and a bi-monthly magazine but it is filling a big gap and making owners more conscious of a lot of things to do with their cars that they might otherwise not know.

R.N. How would you sum up the enjoyment you get from driving your Morris Minor.

J.F. When I slide into the seat behind that split screen it's like being in the cockpit of an aeroplane. I enjoy the additional power in my own car — I enjoy being able to corner just as fast and drive just as quick as modern cars. I enjoy the camaraderie which exists between Morris Minor owners and — wait for it — I adore those semaphore indicators.

R.N. What advice would you give to potential buyers of Morris Minors.

J.F. I would give a very strong word of warning. If you don't know a great deal about Morris Minors then find someone who does and take them with you when you go to look at the vehicle. Always examine the underside of the car meticulously and don't be rushed into making a hasty decision you may live to regret.

BUYING

Which Model?

Anyone contemplating buying a Morris Minor can at least view the prospect with a fair degree of optimism. Allowing for the fact that a large proportion of the early models were exported, there are sufficient numbers left of the 1.6 million produced to permit a reasonable degree of choice. The Morris Minor seems to have outlasted many of its contemporaries and the fact that it is still a common sight on British roads is encouraging to any potential buyer.

An essential pre-requisite to any purchase is a decision on which body style and model to have. Fortunately the Morris Minor range is diverse enough to cater for most tastes. Whether you are looking for the joys of open air motoring or a medium sized estate car or simply a small saloon which comfortably seats four people then, as the publicity information used to say — "There's room for the family in a Morris Minor — The Worlds Biggest Small Car Buy!"

The contemporary B.M.C. promotional sales literature understandably plugged the virtues of the various Morris Minor models and many of the claims made are still relevant to today's Morris Minor buyer even though the small car market has changed dramatically following the advent of the hatchback. Nevertheless there are few who would claim that the Morris Minor was ever a luxury car. Despite its character and charm, it was, and still is for many, a functional vehicle, devoid of frills, with good handling and reasonable performance.

In the case of the Series II vehicles (1952-56) the performance from the 803cc ohv engine was adequate in its day but the choice of gear ratios for this model was subsequently criticised in the motoring press. While they remain vehicles of character, reminiscent of the earlier Morris Minor and, typified by the split windscreen, small rear screen, deep cut rear wings and semaphore indicators, the Series II vehicles lack the acceleration and performance needed for carefree, relaxed everyday motoring in the 1980s. The fact that mechanical and body parts are significantly different from the later "1000" models and are now difficult to obtain has resulted more and more in these vehicles being bought by enthusiasts and collectors.

The 948cc Morris 1000 models (1956-62) are a much better proposition for use as everyday vehicles. The restyled body and the increased performance combined to make this the best selling Morris Minor of them all. Body parts are still available but some difficulty may be experienced in obtaining new components for some of the major mechanical items. It's worth bearing in mind that over twenty five years have elapsed since the 948cc was introduced!

Without doubt the best buy from a realistic and practical point of view is the later 1098cc Morris 1000. Introduced in 1962, this model was updated in subsequent years before finally being discontinued in 1971. Its larger engine boosted acceleration times and increased the top speed, while later styling features increased comfort and safety. Spares for these later vehicles are easy to obtain at present. The fact that many components are shared with other B.L. 1100 A-series engines should ensure a good supply of mechanical parts for some time yet. The current boom in Morris Minor Specialists is reassuring and the knowledge that more and more parts are being manufactured to original specification under the auspices of B.L. Heritage and distributed by firms such as the Morris Minor Centre, Bath, takes some of the risk out of buying a Morris Minor today.

The current trend towards 'converting' saloons into convertibles means that in future prospective buyers would do well to examine the identification code on the chassis plate, as explained earlier, in order to make sure they are buying 'a genuine' convertible.

Historical value patterns

The image of the Morris Minor has changed somewhat over recent years. While it is undoubtedly still a reliable, economical, utilitarian vehicle it has come to be regarded by some people as a "cult" car and by others as a "Postwar Classic Car." Consequently its prestige has increased and unfortunately for potential buyers so have the asking prices.

Such was not always the case. When it was introduced in 1948, the two door Morris Minor sold for £358. 10s. 7d. Twenty years later the price for a similar model was £636 inclusive of Purchase Tax, while the traveller, the most expensive model of the range, sold for £713 inclusive of Purchase Tax.

Over the years prices in the second hand market have

fluctuated tremendously, with Traveller prices generally remaining slightly higher than those of Saloons. Convertibles have tended to command good prices due mainly to the popular demand there is for them and to the fact that there are not so many of them around.

Current prices vary enormously and are governed, as one would expect, largely by age, condition and mileage. It is possible to find one owner examples in excellent condition at reasonable prices — but they do take some finding.

For those who wonder about the worth of their prized possession, or their intended purchase, ponder on this ... In 1974, a privately commissioned Morris 1000 two door Saloon was built from new parts by Dutton Forshaw of Swindon for the Law family. The total cost of this car, including labour, was £3,600.

Problem areas

Only the problem areas which are specific to Morris Minors are covered here: the prospective buyer would do well to check for those general problems which can be found in any car, such as clutch and gearbox wear, a tired or noisy engine, poor brakes or indecisive steering — all items which can be assessed during a careful test drive.

Longevity has become the hallmark of Morris Minor engines and elsewhere in this book consideration is given to their performance and to spare part availability. The rack and pinion steering lasts for a long time too, if carefully maintained. The same applies to the steering swivel pin assemblies, but the ultimate penalty for lack of maintenance here is the depressing sight, often seen, of a Morris Minor with one

of its wheels tucked under the front suspension.

Brakes on Morris Minors have often been criticised and they should be carefully checked before any purchase is made, particularly if the vehicle is known to have been standing for some time. a really hard brake pedal may indicate siezed wheel cylinders while a lack of pressure may denote something more serious. It's worth noting that the brake master cylinder is situated under the floor in a relatively inaccessible place and does present some difficulty for repair. Brake parts for later models are readily available but parts for Series II vehicles are different and may take longer to find.

Gearbox problems are not unknown in Morris Minors. Problems, when they do occur — they are more common in earlier models — usually take the form of excessive noise in first or reverse gears, weak synchromesh and a tendency to jump out of gear. The fact that in the majority of cases, specialist help will have to be sought to rectify these faults, is worth bearing in mind when considering the asking price.

The problem areas most commonly encountered on Morris Minors, and the most serious, are those associated with bodywork. The most obvious areas which are prone to rust are the external panels — front wings rust near to the front door line and around the headlamps while rear wings rust around the beading close to the main body. The bottom edges of rear wings, doors and the boot lid are all areas in which serious rusting occurs. Obtaining replacement panels for Morris 1000 models is not much of a problem, however original Series II body panels are difficult to find and in the case of rear wings enthusiasts keen to retain originality may have to compromise and have later "1000" wings reshaped.

Less obvious but more critical are the structural areas on the

underside of the vehicles which are prone to rusting. These include the front chassis members, the central crossmembers and the jacking points each side of the car, the rear spring hanger mounting points and the floor pan itself. Meticulous probing of these areas will pay dividends in the end. If serious corrosion exists then it might be best to pass and look for another vehicle. Replacement parts and repair panels are readily available from specialists but effecting the repairs can be time consuming and expensive.

Traveller models have additional problems to those already mentioned. The external woodwork is an essential structural component of the vehicle and as such it is an M.o.T. check point. Rotten panels will eventually have to be replaced and although several firms provide a comprehensive woodwork spares service, replacing Traveller wood is an intricate, time consuming and potentially expensive undertaking.

Interior & Exterior Trim

The condition of the interior of the vehicle is a point sometimes overlooked by intending purchasers — often to their cost! For anyone intending to replace interior trim and retain originality the following points are worth bearing in mind.

On early vehicles, the leather seat facing should be carefully examined for splits and tears — leather is always expensive to replace, and the condition of the carpets should be noted. While a variety of firms will supply carpet sets in a range of materials, the original 'Carvel' type carpet is no longer available.

Seat coverings and door trims on 948cc and 1098cc models were fitted in what can only be described as a large range of colours and styles — many of which are no longer available from recognised stockists though the Morris Minor Centre, Bath, does stock the heat-formed vinyl type coverings fitted to later models.

Headlinings should be carefully examined too. Availability isn't much of a problem though they are expensive to replace and tricky to fit.

Well used front seats have a tendency to sag due to worn or broken webbing straps underneath. Repairs can be easily carried out by putting in new straps and in the case of driver's seats, this is often more practical than simply swapping for a less 'saggy' passenger seat, which will be slightly out of alignment anyway when it is fitted to the driver's side.

Exterior trim, particularly chromework, can prove expensive and difficult to replace. Most of the chromework on Morris Minors is subject to pitting after a period of time. The base metal 'Masak' often referred to as 'Monkey metal' is difficult to repolish in preparation for replating. Consequently replating firms are reluctant to rechrome items such as badges, door handles and hinges. Finding new chrome parts can prove difficult, particularly for

Series II cars, but private individuals, the Morris Minor Centre, Bath and the Morris Minor Owners' Club are endeavouring to fill the gap.

Summing-up

Anyone wishing to purchase a Morris Minor can do so at the present time in the knowledge that enough of them are advertised in the motoring and local press to allow a fair degree of choice. They can approach their purchase with the reassurance that there are sufficient specialist firms around to help keep their vehicle on the road for some time to come and that advice and guidance can be obtained by joining an established Morris Minor car club.

Those wishing to purchase a vehicle with complete or partial restoration in mind can do so knowing that its all been done before — and, in the case of one Saloon, fully documented over a two year period in the monthly magazine *Practical Classics*. For those to whom money is no object, there are specialist firms who will carry out complete restorations to individual requirements - at a price!

CLUBS, SPECIALISTS & BOOKS

Now that over a decade has passed since the last Morris Minor left the production line, the need for specialist help and advice assumes, and will continue to assume, increasing importance. A testimony to this fact is the ever increasing membership of Morris Minor car clubs and the growing number of specialist firms providing services which range from the manufacture of specific parts to full restoration.

This section considers some of the owners clubs, specialist firms and publications which the author feels may be of interest to Morris Minor owners. It should be noted that in the case of specialist firms, the list is only representative of the services offered, and has been compiled by the author on the basis of recommendation or personal contact — this does not mean that there are not other equally proficient specialists dotted around the world.

Morris Minor Owners Club

Established in 1977, this fast growing national club provides a wide ranging service for its large membership. Contact is maintained via a well produced and informative bi-monthly magazine *Minor Matters*, by informal monthly meetings at twenty nine regional branches and by branch, regional and national rallies and events. The club also provides technical advice and a comprehensive spares service for members. Other benefits include negotiated discounts on certain spares, services and insurance.
Club contact: Jill Holmes, Membership Secretary, 10 Stowe View, Tingewick, Buckinghamshire, England.

North East Morris Minor Club

A club of some three hundred members which meets monthly and provides its members with a monthly newsletter and a useful spares service. Actively supported local rallies and events and has negotiated discounts for members.
Club contact: Samantha Davey, 9 Hatfield Place, Peterlee, Co. Durham, England.

Cornwall Morris 1000 Club

Billed as the Club for Morris Minor owners West of the Tamar, this club with 200 members produces a monthly newsletter, operates a second hand spares service and provides the opportunity for members to meet.
Club contact: Alan James, 10 Polstain Road, Threemilestone, Truro, Cornwall, England.

Morris Minor Registry/Morris Owners Association of California

Over the years there have been a number of American clubs for Morris Minors. The first was formed with the help of the B.M.C. Sales organisation in the mid-50s but this folded after a few years. The two clubs which are in existence at present operated for a time unaware of each other. They remain independent but co-produce a monthly magazine called *Minor News*.
Morris Minor Registry/Morris Owners Association of California, 2311 30th Avenue, San Francisco, CA94116, USA.

Other Clubs

Amicale Morris Minor, Pierre Gravel, 37 Bis Rue Bourbon, 37120 Richelieu, France.
Morris Minor Club Nederland, J.A. de Bruyne, Voorzitter Noldijk 67, Barendrecht 01806-3586, Holland.
Nordisk Morris Minor Klubb, Box 37, Houseter, Oslo 37.
Morris Minor Registret, Laduvägen 1 S-78134, Borlänge, Sweden.
Morris Minor Group of British Columbia, c/o No.1 1957 McNicoll Ave., Vancouver BC V6J1A7, Canada.
Morris Minor Car Club of New Zealand. Stan Hunte, 35 Hayr Road, Mount Roskill, Auckland, New Zealand.
Morris Minor Car Club of Victoria, Robert Mackie, 12 Fairhills Parade, Glen Waverley 3150, Australia.
Morris Minor Car Club of New South Wales, P.O. Box 151, Earlwood 2206, Australia.
Morris Minor Car Club of Western Australia, 86 Richmond Street, Leederville 6007, Australia.
Morris Minor Club, South Africa, G.R. Dodds, 44 Fordyce Road, Walmer 6065, Port Elizabeth, South Africa.

Specialists

The Morris Minor Centre, Avon House, Lower Bristol Road, Bath, England. Spares Dept., Unit 5, Locksbrook, Avon Trading Estate, Bath, England. Sole B.L. Heritage parts supplier. Complete range of services including full restoration.

Morris Minor East Midlands, 71 Uppingham Road, Houghton on the Hill, Leicester, England. Suppliers of Morris Minor Centre spares. Special interest in Series II models. Restorations undertaken. Over the counter and mail order service.

John Black (Fenton) Limited, Premier Garage, Victoria Road, Fenton, Stoke on Trent ST4 2LJ, England. Morris Minor Centre approved parts supplier. Specialist workshop for mechanical and bodywork repairs.

Woodwork Supplies, Stedham Sawmills, Stedham, Nr. Midhurst, West Sussex GU29 ONY, England. Replacement body panels, woodwork, trim and accessories for Minor 1000 and Traveller.

R.G. Plant, Unit 16, Crawley Mills Industrial Estate, Crawley, Nr. Witney, Oxon, England. Specialist interest in Morris Minors. Resprays a speciality.

The Don Trimming Co. Ltd., Hampton Road, Erdington, Birmingham B23 7JJ, England. Convertible Hoods supplied and fitted, also carpets, upholstery and trim.

Henric, Lortas Road, New Basford, Nottingham, England. Manufacturers and suppliers of replacement and repair panels.

Woolies (Ian Caroline Woolstenholmes Ltd.), off Blenheim Way, Northfields Industrial Estate, Market Deeping, Peterborough PE6 8CD, England. This company specialises in items of trim.

Paul Beck, Vintage Supplies, High Street, Stalham, Norwich, Norfolk NR12 9BB, England. Another company specialising in items of trim.

MORRISERVICE. 120 Fifth Avenue, Redwood City, CA 94016, USA. Largest stockist of Morris Minor parts in North America, based in California.

Books

Morris Minor 1000 Owners Handbook
Haynes Publishing Group.
Covers models from 1956-71, 948cc and 1098cc. Easy to follow guide.

Morris Minor 1000 Owners Workshop Manual
Haynes Publishing Group.
Covers all models from 1956-71, 948cc and 1098cc. Well illustrated manual with useful fault finding sections.

Morris Minor: The World's Supreme Small Car, by Paul Skilleter. Osprey.
An award winning publication which amongst other things gives a comprehensive account of the origins and development of the whole range of Morris Minor vehicles.

Morris Minor 1948-70, by R.M. Clarke.
Brookland Books.
A collection of articles, road tests and buying features, compiled in chronological order, which give an insight into contemporary views. Rather like the Road Test section of this publication.

Morris Minor Collection
Brookland Books.
To be published in July 1982. Collected contemporary comment and road tests.

The Morris Minor: Purchase and Restoration, by Roger Bateman.
A concise informative booklet for the prospective buyer or restorer. Available from: R. Bateman, 1 Heath View, East End, Lymington, Hants.

Morris Minor (including Minor 1000, Series II and Series MM)
Pearson's Illustrated Car Servicing for Owner Drivers, by D.V.W.Francis.
Hamlyn Publishing Group.
A very useful publication especially for owners of early models, thought to be no longer in print but second hand examples should be available.

PHOTO GALLERY

1

2

3

1. First prototype, the "Mosquito", dating from 1943, Code EX/3X/86, with narrower body than eventual production model and significantly different front grille arrangement. (B.L.Heritage.)

2. 1947 Mosquito on test. All eight of the pre-production prototypes underwent thorough testing. Later ones were fitted with an experimental flat four engine, but this never went into production. (B.L.Heritage.)

3. Series M.M. 4 door saloon of the 1952 variety and sporting headlamps in the wings. Earlier M.Ms, the "lowlight" models, had the lights in the grille panel. The change to headlamps in wings reduced the top speed by 1½ mph!

4. An early Series II saloon. Exterior features show little change from the M.M., the only identifying feature being the bonnet motif, which replaced the 'flash', and the new pointed badge. Clearly seen is the 4 inch flat strip running through the centre of the bonnet — a legacy of widening the "Mosquito"!

5. Rear view of same, showing no change from the earlier M.M. Note the small rear screen and the (concession to safety?) unusually placed trafficators.

4

5

6. A feature of earlier Morris Minors was the deep cut rear wings now virtually unobtainable in original form. Later "1000" wings can be reshaped however.

7. Early Series II engine bay showing 803cc power unit and accessories. Points of interest include the curved bulkhead panel to the rear of the engine — a modification needed to allow the new engine unit clearance — the position of the coil and the cumbersome air cleaner arrangement.

8. A later Series II engine bay showing a number of changes. Unlike the earlier version this model is not fitted with a heater, the position of the coil has changed — as has the arrangement for the air cleaner.

9. The later Series IIs had horizontal grille bars and the sidelights were moved to the wings.

10. Rear lights changed too, though everything else to the rear of the car remained the same.

11. The early Series II interior was almost identical to that of the M.M. Points of interest here are, the separate fuel, oil pressure and speedometer gauges, mottled type steering wheel, trafficator switch and the straight gearlever — characteristic of the 803cc models.

12. Access to the rear seat in 2 door saloons was facilitated by a forward tipping driver's seat.

13. Under fascia view showing early type circulatory heater available for Series II vehicles. Note, too, the useful parcel shelf.

14. Later Series II interior showing the new style fascia with central control panel, open gloveboxes and repositioned ashtray.

15. First introduced in 1953 the Traveller was destined to be a popular model. This is a later Series II model. Note the stainless steel window surround, the over riders and the inevitable, owner added, flashing indicators. (Roy Turner.)

11

12

13

14

15

16

17

18

19

20

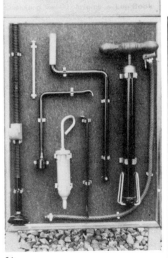

21

16. Series II Convertible. The angular hood contrasts sharply with the unique rounded styling features of the body.

17. Overhead view showing the definitive lines of the early type canvas hood. "It's never been down in twenty-seven years" the owner said!

18. Threequarter view of the same Convertible suggesting possibilities of restricted vision through the rear with the hood up.

19. "They don't make them like that any more!" They do, at a price — but this one has stood the test of time.

20. The 7 cu.ft. of luggage space was always a promotional point on Morris Minor sales literature. On all cars the rear seat folded down to provide additional space for awkward items.

21. Something to put in that cavernous boot? Every Morris Minor owner should have a tool kit — but it is unlikely to be as complete as this 1955 Series II original set . . .

22

23

24

25

22. A chance to compare a later Series M.M. with the new look. Morris Minor 1000 introduced in 1956. Bid farewell to the split screen, say welcome to a restyled range with many new features.

23 & 24. The new model sported a new boot badge, and a new bonnet motif replacing the earlier Morris Minor variety.

25. The Traveller continued in production and benefited from improved interior fittings, including contrasting piping on upholstery, reminiscent of some of the Austin range. (B.L.Heritage.)

26 & 27. One of the main styling changes for the Morris 1000 was the increase in the size of the front and rear screens. The benefit in increased visibility is clearly illustrated in these comparison pictures. Note also the improved access to the rear seat on the later 2 door saloon and the addition of an ashtray in the rear.

26

27

28

30

29

31

28. The improved rear seat accessibility of the "1000" from the passenger side was due mainly to the more compact folding of the front seat shown here.

29 & 30. The 2 door saloon was the most popular model of all the Morris Minors. This example shows very well the restyled features which helped make the 948cc version of the Morris Minor the best selling of them all. They include the larger front and rear screens, new style rear wings and restyled rear lights. The indicators are non-original.

31. The 948cc model was the one which sold best in the United States. Seen here is the L.H.D. Fascia panel layout. The only draw back — and an irritating one at that — was the absence of a lock in the left hand door. Foreign drivers had to get into their vehicles from the righthand (passenger) side! (B.L.Heritage.)

32. American 2 door sedan, 1959, owned by Bob Theida, Illinois. The car is finished in red and has a white interior. (Minor News.)

32

33. The more conventional R.H.D. of the 948cc "1000" layout showing the new steering wheel, lidded glove compartments and the new style shortened gearlever. The simplicity of the layout pleased many but some questioned the value of the lidded glove compartment behind the steering wheel.

34. Under fascia view of the same car showing the new style heater shroud and bonnet release pull. The foot controls and foot operated head light dip switch are also shown.

35. The engine compartment of the 948cc Morris 1000. Compact, functional and pleasing to look at. An A-series engine of proven reliability.

36, 37 & 38. Semaphore indicators were a feature of all early models. They could be troublesome and temperamental. Two positions were adopted: the lower side panel on 2 door models and the upper door pillar on 4 door and Traveller models. The latter position is still identifiable on the upper door posts of later 1000 models.

39. A 1961 Morris 1000 948cc convertible in a typically British setting. Interestingly it is one of the first vehicles not fitted with semaphore indicators. It sports a B.M.C. rosette on the windscreen — a reminder of the formation of the British Motor Corporation in 1952 following the amalgamation of the Austin Motor Company and the Nuffield Organisation. (B.L.Heritage.)

33

34

35

36

37

38

39

40. One of the limited range of 349 vehicles launched in January 1961 to mark the production of the millionth Morris Minor. Note the special ''1,000,000'' side bonnet badge and the special wheel rim embellishers. The best remaining example is owned by a Wolverhampton Garage, Bradburn & Wedge Ltd, and has, at the time of writing, 1367 miles on the clock. American interest in these vehicles is high and John Voelcker of the Morris Minor Registry is compiling a Register of remaining examples. (B.L.Heritage.)

41, 42 & 43. Views of the revamped post-1962 Morris 1000 saloon. This model featuring the additional changes of October 1965.

44. The 1098cc engine and accessories. This, the final and largest standard power unit fitted to the Morris Minor, provided increased performance yet retained excellent economy. The bay is characterised by the new fresh air heater duct tube and yet another restyled air cleaner fitment.

45. 14 inch road wheels were used throughout production on all Morris Minors in spite of the doubts the technical experts expressed in pre-production days when larger wheels were the norm.

46. The front suspension, shown here, remained virtually unchanged throughout production; This is a testimony to its successful design. The box section to the right of the picture running down the car and the ''tie plate'' — yes those holes are supposed to be there! — are common rust spots.

40

41

42

43

45

46

44

47. Final interior fittings of later 1088cc Morris 1000 saloon. Features include dished steering wheel, open glovebox on drivers side, redesigned control panel complete with windscreen washer button, indicator stalk with flasher and swivel ashtrays each side of parcel shelf.

48. Interior view of 4 door saloon showing heat formed upholstery and door trim panels. Other points of interest include the seatbelt mounting points and the door pulls — which on the front doors have a limited life expectancy!

49. A variety of seat belt arrangements were fitted to Morris Minors. This unusual fitting was standard equipment on a 1966 four door Saloon.

50. In this setting the convertible is very much at home.

51. Talking of home! Hood down? Why not? The sun does shine — some of the time. Now what did the manual say? Release the wing bolts attaching the forward end of the hood to the head rail. Raise the hood upwards and backwards and then fold so that the sticks lie on top of each other. Make sure no material is trapped between the sticks. Fold the hood making sure there are no creases and tuck the corners in . . .

47

48

50

49

51

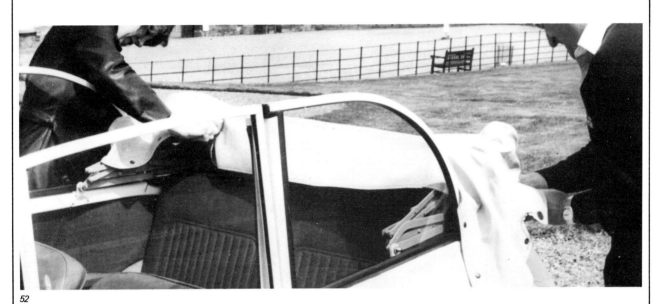

52

53

54

57

52. ... withdraw the hood cover and fit over the folded hood; fasten in position using the press studs ...

53. ... easy when you know how, isn't it?

54. Now isn't that a smart job?

55. Distinctive rear light fitting of later cars, which combines amber lens and brake light.

56. Front lighting arrangement. Combined side light indicator unit plus sealed beam headlights on later home market models.

57. Improved wipers, with larger sweep and 'tandem' action as opposed to 'clap hands' action of earlier models, were fitted from 1963.

55

56

58 & 59. Front and side views of 1968 Morris 1000 Traveller which exhibits some interesting modifications.

60. Interior view of same Traveller showing the 40 cu.ft. of luggage space which made it such a versatile vehicle. Points of interest are the automatic locking check device on the rear doors, the large sliding side windows which allowed for better ventilation and the excellent all round visibility.

61. Rear view showing the 20 cu.ft. of luggage space available with the rear seat in position and the concealed spare wheel compartment, so useful for storing tools etc. This is a working vehicle — as it was originally designed to be and extras include tow bar, reversing and brake lights.

58

59

60

61

62. Morris Minor brakes have been the subject of criticism from time to time. Modifications like this can lead to improved ride and more stopping power. This view shows the Riley 1.5 brake drum of 9 inch diameter, a Koni telescopic shock absorber with its top mounting bracket bolted to the inner wing.

63. This view shows the Koni telescopic shock absorber bottom mounting bracket which is clamped onto the bottom wishbone assembly. There is a boss on the far side of the wishbone which takes the bottom eye of the shock absorber

(similar to the top). The Riley 1.5 flexible brake hose is used.

64. Koni telescopic shock absorber conversion to rear suspension. The conversion bracket replaces the normal U-bolt bottom plate shock absorber mount.

65. Reclining seats were available as an optional extra on later cars but only for the driver's seat. This unusual shot shows that two reclining seats can be fitted. The seats recline in 5 positions. Other optional extras included whitewall types and Dunlop SP41 tyres. (Ted Hunt.)

66 & 67. Steering column ignition locks were fitted to late Traveller models and Morris Minor commercials as shown here. A blank space resulted on the central control panel where previously the ignition key was inserted. (66/Roy Turner.)

68. An unregistered Morris Minor belonging to Ken Smith who lives in Dublin. It has 118 miles on the clock and is unmarked. The car was built by G.A. Brittain Ltd., the Irish Assemblers of Morris Minors, in 1971. (Joe Melia.)

62

63

64

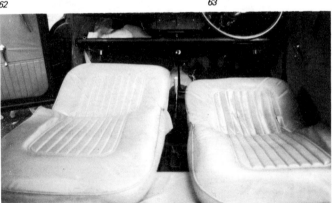

65

66

67

68

69, 70 & 71. Beware - rust! Typical corrosion
points are around the headlamp, the back of the
front wing and central crossmember/jacking point.
Proper repairs will be expensive and time
consuming — and it is very unlikely that these will
be the only effected areas in a neglected vehicle.
(Paul Skilleter.)

72. Pat Moss (interviewee in the "Owner's View
section) and Anne Wisdom in action with
"Grannie" in the Liege-Rome-Liege of 1957. They
finished 23rd overall and took second place in the
Coupe des Dames. (Pat Carlsson.)

73. David Burrows winner of Class D in the 1981
Pre-57 Saloon Car Championship of Gt. Britain
seen here having a tussle with one of his rivals in
a Standard 10. (Fred Scatley.)

74. Jim Funnell interviewee in the Owner's View
section seen here entering Woodcote, Silverstone,
while competing with an early version of his
Morris Minor/Ford Special, during 1980. (Harold
Barker.)

69

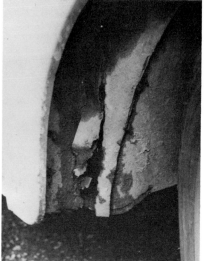

70

71

72

73

74

C1.

C1. This 1954 Series II is an interesting example. It has completed 110,000 miles and has been brought up to this standard by patient hardwork over a number of years. Showing that it can be done! A feature worth noting is the painted grille panel complete with sidelights and the painted metal window surround common to all two door Saloons.

C2. 1955 Series II Convertible with original canvas hood. A striking example of this model which is in original condition inside and out. Finished in Clarendon Grey it has a contrasting red interior. The original tool kit illustrated earlier (21) belongs to this vehicle.

C2.

C3.   Front interior view of 1955 Series II
Convertible showing the new style fascia panel.
Compared to the earlier Series II and M.M. fascia
it was spartan and lacked character. Detail points
worth noting are the position of the semaphore
indicators, the leather door pulls, large early type
handbrake and original type "carvel" carpet, now
unobtainable.

C4.   For those who've asked, "What's it like in
the back of a convertible?" Here is the answer.
The fold away front passenger seat allows easy
access to the rear seat of this 1955 Series II
Convertible. The starkness of the hood sticks,
which were visible when the hood was up, was a
bit off-putting to some people.

C3.

C4.

C5.

C6.

C7.

C5. One of the last Series II four door Saloons, manufactured in 1956, and finished in an unusual colour — Sage Green. The contrasting wheel rims give a pleasing effect.

C6. Engine compartment of 1956 Series II model. In contrast to the engine bay shown earlier in monochrome section (8) this model has a heater fitted (the hoses leading to the control valve at the rear of the engine block are clearly shown). The engine steady bar can also be seen.

C7. Series II Traveller. A rare breed as they say. This one belongs to Adrian Bartlett who organises a Series II Traveller register. So far he has managed to track down 70, of these 21 in the U.S.A., 5 in Australia, 3 in Canada and 41 in the U.K. (Roy Turner.)

C8.

C8.   Proving that one lady owner, low mileage vehicles are not just salesmen's pipedreams, this fine 1960 948cc two door Saloon was bought with less than 30,000 miles on the clock. It is finished in Clipper Blue, a distinctive colour, and is immaculate.

C9.   Interior fittings on this 1960 948cc model do little to provide contrast to the overwhelming blueness. The only concessions are a white fabric covering on the parcel shelf lip, and stainless steel edging on the glove compartment boxes. It is difficult to believe that this car is over twenty years old!

C10.   The engine bay of the same 1960 948cc Saloon is compact and functional and is certainly much less cluttered in appearance than that of its 1098cc successor.

C9.

C10.

C11.

C12.

C13.

C11. Engine bay of the later cars. Despite encroachment due to additional components being introduced the engine bay remained roomy and permitted easy access for repair and maintenance purposes. (Roy Turner.)

C12. This stunning white convertible is an exceptionally good example of the model in its final form. A top award winning car with accolades like ''Car of the Show'' at the 1981 Classic Car Show Brighton.

C13. And then there were three! Saloon, Traveller and Convertible. The Convertible was the first to be discontinued, followed by the Saloons. Fittingly the Traveller which was the last to be introduced was the last to leave production.

C14. *Just like the sales brochure! This overhead photograph shows very well the interior appointment of the later cars. Points worth noting are the crushable sun visors and hood fittings on the front rail and the seatbelt arrangement common to all two door models.*

C15. *One of the last two door saloons. The two door model was the most prolific of all models. The first Morris Minor in production NWL 576 was a two door saloon and the last saloon to leave the production line at Cowley on 12th November 1970 was also a 2 door. (Roy Turner.)*

C14.

C15.

C16 & 17. 1966. Four door saloon showing to good effect the classic lines of the 1098cc models (Series 5) and the distinctive much improved lighting/indicator arrangement.

C16

C17.

C18.

C18. Not for purists — but Morris Minor enthusiasm takes many forms. ''Blue for You'' illustrates just how well the Minor's shape lends itself to customising. (Paul Davies.)

C19. Picking up her skirts and flying — the 1980 Himalayan Rally Morris 1000 Saloon formerly owned by the Archbishop of Canterbury, but shown in unfamiliar territory. Driven by Philip Young and the Rev. Rupert Jones it finished first in its class and fifteenth overall in spite of starting in 67th place. (Copyright Philip Young.)

C20. A field full of Minors and 1000s! Joining one of the recognised clubs has untold benefits for Morris Minor and 1000 owners. Gatherings like this are regular occurances during the Summer months for members of the Morris Minor Owners Club. An opportunity is afforded to meet old friends and make new ones, to buy, sell or swop spares, and to appreciate other people's cars. The car in the foreground is the first production Minor. (Michael Moore.)

C19.

C20.